Working Papers

Chapters 1-17

Accounting 24e, Financial Accounting 12e, or Accounting Using Excel for Success 2e

Carl S. Warren
Professor Emeritus of Accounting
University of Georgia, Athens

James M. Reeve
Professor Emeritus of Accounting
University of Tennessee, Knoxville

Jonathan E. Duchac
Professor of Accounting
Wake Forest University

SOUTH-WESTERN
CENGAGE Learning

Australia • Brazil • Japan • Korea • Mexico • Singapore • Spain • United Kingdom • United States

ISBN-13: 978-0-538-47853-3
ISBN-10: 0-538-47853-5

South-Western Cengage Learning
5191 Natorp Boulevard
Mason, OH 45040
USA

Cengage Learning is a leading provider of customized learning solutions with office locations around the globe, including Singapore, the United Kingdom, Australia, Mexico, Brazil, and Japan. Locate your local office at: **international.cengage.com/region**.

Cengage Learning products are represented in Canada by Nelson Education, Ltd.

For your course and learning solutions, visit **www.cengage.com**.

Purchase any of our products at your local college store or at our preferred online store **www.CengageBrain.com**.

READ IMPORTANT LICENSE INFORMATION

Printed in the United States of America
1 2 3 4 5 6 7   14 13 12 11 10

CONTENTS

1	Introduction to Accounting and Business	1
2	Analyzing Transactions	37
3	The Adjusting Process	95
4	Completing the Accounting Cycle	125
5	Accounting Systems	225
6	Accounting for Merchandising Businesses	277
7	Inventories	347
8	Sarbanes-Oxley, Internal Control, and Cash	371
9	Receivables	399
10	Fixed Assets and Intangible Assets	431
11	Current Liabilities and Payroll	455
12	Accounting for Partnerships and Limited Liability Companies	497
13	Corporations: Organization, Stock Transactions, and Dividends	537
14	Long-Term Liabilities: Bonds and Notes	565
15	Investments and Fair Value Accounting	593
16	Statement of Cash Flows	637
17	Financial Statement Analysis	669
App. B	Reversing Entries	709
App. D	International Financial Reporting Standards	moved to online

The working papers include problem-specific forms for preparing solutions for Exercises, A&B Problems, the Continuing Problem, and the Comprehensive Problems from the textbook. These forms, with preprinted headings, provide a structure for the problems, which will help you get started and save you time.

Based on students' testimonials and instructors' feedback, the forms in the working papers have been streamlined to make them simpler to use and to better reflect the changing environment of business. For example, the vertical rules that separated digits of numbers entered into journals, ledgers, and statements have been removed, making it easier to write in numbers.

Note that when entering whole amounts into the forms, your instructor will direct you on whether to include a decimal point and zeroes (e.g., 100.00) or to omit those (e.g., 100).

EXERCISE 1-1

a.

1. _____   6. _____   11. _____
2. _____   7. _____   12. _____
3. _____   8. _____   13. _____
4. _____   9. _____   14. _____
5. _____   10. _____   15. _____

b.

_____

_____

_____

EXERCISE 1-2

_____

_____

_____

_____

_____

_____

EXERCISE 1-3

a.

1. _____   6. _____
2. _____   7. _____
3. _____   8. _____
4. _____   9. _____
5. _____   10. _____

b.

_____

_____

_____

EXERCISE 1-4

_____

_____

EXERCISE 1-5

_____

_____

EXERCISE 1-6

	Assets	=	Liabilities	+	Owner's Equity
a.	_____	=	$150,000	+	$450,000
b.	$275,000	=	_____	+	$50,000
c.	$615,000	=	$190,000	+	_____

EXERCISE 1-7

a. _____

b. _____

c. _____

d. _____

e. _____

EXERCISE 1-8

a. _____

b. _____

c. _____

d. _____

e. _____

f. _____

EXERCISE 1-9

a. _____

b. _____

c. _____

d. _____

e. _____

EXERCISE 1-10

a. (1) Assets: _____

   (2) Liabilities: _____

   (3) Owner's equity: _____

b. (1) Assets: _____

   (2) Liabilities: _____

   (3) Owner's equity: _____

c.

_____

_____

_____

EXERCISE 1-11

1. Owner's investments: _____

2. Revenues: _____

3. Expenses: _____

4. Owner's withdrawals: _____

EXERCISE 1-12

1. _____   6. _____

2. _____   7. _____

3. _____   8. _____

4. _____   9. _____

5. _____   10. _____

EXERCISE 1-13

a. (1) _____

   (2) _____

   (3) _____

   (4) _____

   (5) _____

   (6) _____

   (7) _____

b. _____

c. _____

d. _____

e. _____

EXERCISE 1-14

_____

_____

_____

_____

_____

_____

_____

EXERCISE 1-15

Aries:		
Gemini:		
Leo:		
Pisces:		

EXERCISE 1-16

  1. Accounts Receivable: _____

  2. Cash: _____

  3. Fees Earned: _____

  4. Land: _____

  5. Patsy Adkins, Capital: _____

  6. Supplies: _____

  7. Supplies Expense: _____

  8. Utilities Expense: _____

  9. Wages Expense: _____

10. Wages Payable: _____

EXERCISE 1-17

  1. Accounts Receivable: _____

  2. Cash: _____

  3. Fees Earned: _____

  4. Land: _____

  5. Patsy Adkins, Capital: _____

  6. Supplies: _____

  7. Supplies Expense: _____

  8. Utilities Expense: _____

  9. Wages Expense: _____

10. Wages Payable: _____

EXERCISE 1-18

a.

Statement of Owner's Equity

EXERCISE 1-18, Concluded

b.

_____

_____

_____

EXERCISE 1-19

Income Statement		

EXERCISE   1-20

Aquarius:		
Libra:		
Scorpio:		
Taurus:		

EXERCISE 1-21

a.

	Balance Sheet		

	Balance Sheet		

b.	
c.	

EXERCISE 1-22

a.

  1. Accounts payable: _____

  2. Cash equivalents: _____

  3. Crude oil inventory: _____

  4. Equipment: _____

  5. Exploration expenses: _____

  6. Income taxes payable: _____

  7. Investments: _____

  8. Long-term debt: _____

  9. Marketable securities: _____

10. Notes and loans payable: _____

11. Notes receivable: _____

12. Operating expenses: _____

13. Prepaid taxes: _____

14. Sales: _____

15. Selling expenses: _____

b.

_____

_____

_____

c.

_____

_____

_____

EXERCISE 1-23

1. Cash received from fees earned: _____

2. Cash paid for expenses: _____

3. Cash paid for land: _____

4. Cash received as an additional investment by owner: _____

EXERCISE 1-24

Statement of Cash Flows		

EXERCISE 1-25

EXERCISE 1-25, Continued

(optional)

Income Statement

Statement of Owner's Equity

EXERCISE 1-25, Concluded

(optional)

	Balance Sheet		

EXERCISE 1-26

a. _____

_____

b. _____

_____

c. _____

_____

_____

_____

_____

EXERCISE 1-27

a. _____

_____

b. _____

_____

c. _____

_____

_____

_____

d. _____

_____

_____

_____

PROBLEM 1-1 ___

1.

	ASSETS		=	LIABILITIES	+	OWNER'S EQUITY					
Cash	+ Accounts Receivable	+ Supplies	=	Accounts Payable	+ Capital	– Drawing	+ Fees Earned	– Rent Exp.	– Sal. Exp.	– Supp. Exp.	– Auto Exp.	– Misc. Exp.

a.

b.

Bal.

c.

Bal.

d.

Bal.

e.

Bal.

f.

Bal.

g.

Bal.

h.

Bal.

i.

Bal.

j.

Bal.

2.

Name _____

PROBLEM 1-1_, Concluded

3.

4.

PROBLEM 1-2 ___

1.

Income Statement

2.

Statement of Owner's Equity

PROBLEM 1-2 ___ , Concluded

3.

	Balance Sheet		

4. _____

_____

_____

PROBLEM 1-3 ___

1.

	Income Statement		

2.

	Statement of Owner's Equity		

PROBLEM 1-3 ___ , Concluded

3.

	Balance Sheet		

4. (Optional)

	Statement of Cash Flows	

PROBLEM 1-4 ___

1.

	ASSETS		=	LIABILITIES	+				OWNER'S EQUITY					
	Cash	+ Supplies	=	Accounts Payable	+	Capital	− Drawing	+	Sales Comm.	− Rent Exp.	− Office Sal. Exp.	− Auto Exp.	− Supp. Exp.	− Misc. Exp.
a.														
b.														
Bal.														
c.														
Bal.														
d.														
Bal.														
e.														
Bal.														
f.														
Bal.														
g.														
Bal.														
h.														
Bal.														
i.														
Bal.														

PROBLEM 1-4 ___ , Continued

2.

Income Statement

Statement of Owner's Equity

PROBLEM 1-4 ___ , Concluded

Balance Sheet

This Page Not Used.

25

PROBLEM 1-5 ___

1.

Cash	+	Accounts Receivable	+	Supplies	+	Land	=	Accounts Payable	+	Capital	Capital	Capital

ASSETS

LIABILITIES + OWNER'S EQUITY

Name _____

PROBLEM 1-5_____, Continued

2.

	ASSETS				=	LIABILITIES +		OWNER'S EQUITY									
Cash +	Accts. Rec. +	Supplies +	Land =			Accts. Pay.	+ Capital −	Drawing +	Dry Cleaning Revenue −	Dry Cleaning Exp. −	Wages Exp. −	Rent Exp. −	Supp. Exp. −	Truck Exp. −	Util. Exp. −	Misc. Exp.
Bal.																
a.																
Bal.																
b.																
Bal.																
c.																
Bal.																
d.																
Bal.																
e.																
Bal.																
f.																
Bal.																
g.																
Bal.																
h.																
Bal.																
i.																
Bal.																
j.																
Bal.																
k.																
Bal.																
l.																
Bal.																

PROBLEM 1-5 ___ , Continued

3a.

Income Statement

3b.

Statement of Owner's Equity

PROBLEM 1-5 ___, Continued

3c.

	Balance Sheet		

PROBLEM 1-5 ___, Concluded

4. (Optional)

Statement of Cash Flows		

This Page Not Used.

PROBLEM 1-6 ___

a. _____

b. _____

c. _____

d. _____

e. _____

f. _____

g. _____

h. _____

i. _____

j. _____

k. _____

l. _____

m. _____

n. _____

o. _____

p. _____

q. _____

This Page Not Used.

CONTINUING PROBLEM

1.

	ASSETS			=	LIABILITIES +		OWNER'S EQUITY								
	Cash	+	Accts. Rec.	+ Supplies =	Accts. Pay.	+ Pat Sharpe, Capital	− Pat Sharpe, Drawing	+ Fees Earned	− Music Exp.	− Office Rent Exp.	− Equip. Rent Exp.	− Adv. Exp.	− Wages Exp.	− Util. Exp.	− Sup. Exp.	− Misc. Exp.
6/1																
6/2																
Bal.																
6/2																
Bal.																
6/4																
Bal.																
6/6																
Bal.																
6/8																
Bal.																
6/12																
Bal.																
6/13																
Bal.																
6/16																
Bal.																
6/22																
Bal.																
6/25																
Bal.																
6/29																
Bal.																
6/30																
Bal.																

CONTINUING PROBLEM, Continued

1.

	ASSETS		=	LIABILITIES +		OWNER'S EQUITY									
Cash +	Accts. Rec. +	Supplies =		Accts. Pay.	+	Pat Sharpe, Capital –	Pat Sharpe, Drawing +	Fees Earned –	Music Exp. –	Office Rent Exp. –	Equip. Rent Exp. –	Adv. Exp. –	Wages Exp. –	Util. Exp. –	Sup. Exp. –	Misc. Exp.

Bal.

6/30

Bal.

6/30

Bal.

6/30

Bal.

6/30

Bal.

6/30

Bal.

6/30

Bal.

6/30

Bal.

CONTINUING PROBLEM, Continued

2.

Income Statement

3.

Statement of Owner's Equity

CONTINUING PROBLEM, Concluded

4.

Balance Sheet			

EXERCISE 2-1

Accounts Payable: _____

Air Traffic Liability: _____

Aircraft Fuel Expense: _____

Cargo and Mail Revenue: _____

Commissions: _____

Flight Equipment: _____

Landing Fees: _____

Passenger Revenue: _____

Purchase Deposits for Flight Equipment: _____

Spare Parts and Supplies: _____

EXERCISE 2-2

Account	Account Number
Accounts Payable..................	_____
Accounts Receivable.............	_____
Cash	_____
Fees Earned..........................	_____
Jean Cartier, Capital..............	_____
Jean Cartier, Drawing............	_____
Land …………………………..	_____
Miscellaneous Expense …....	_____
Supplies Expense …………....	_____
Wages Expense	_____

EXERCISE 2-3

Balance Sheet Accounts			Income Statement Accounts	
Acct #	**Account Name**		**Acct #**	**Account Name**
	1. Assets			4. Revenue
				5. Expenses
	2. Liabilities			
	3. Owner's Equity			

EXERCISE 2-4

	Increase	Decrease	Normal Balance
Balance sheet accounts:			
Asset.................................	(a) _____	Credit	(b) _____
Liability...............................	Credit	(c) _____	(d) _____
Owner's Equity:			
Capital	Credit	(e) _____	(f) _____
Drawing	(g) _____	(h) _____	(i) _____
Income statement accounts:			
Revenue	Credit	(j) _____	(k) _____
Expense..............................	(l) _____	Credit	Debit

EXERCISE 2-5

1. Accounts Payable: _____

2. Accounts Receivable: _____

3. Cash: _____

4. Fees Earned: _____

5. Insurance Expense: _____

6. Nicki Swanson, Drawing: _____

7. Utilities Expense: _____

EXERCISE 2-6

a. Accounts Payable: _____

b. Accounts Receivable: _____

d. Barbara Mallary, Capital: _____

e. Barbara Mallary, Drawing: _____

c. Cash: _____

f. Fees Earned: _____

g. Office Equipment: _____

h. Rent Expense: _____

i. Supplies: _____

j. Wages Expense: _____

EXERCISE   2-7

JOURNAL PAGE

	DATE	DESCRIPTION	POST. REF.	DEBIT	CREDIT	
1						1
2						2
3						3
4						4
5						5
6						6
7						7
8						8
9						9
10						10
11						11
12						12
13						13
14						14
15						15
16						16
17						17
18						18
19						19
20						20
21						21
22						22
23						23
24						24
25						25
26						26
27						27
28						28
29						29
30						30
31						31
32						32

EXERCISE 2-8

a.

		JOURNAL			PAGE *19*	
	DATE	DESCRIPTION	POST. REF.	DEBIT	CREDIT	
1						1
2						2
3						3
4						4

b., c., d.

ACCOUNT _____ ACCOUNT NO. _____

DATE	ITEM	POST. REF.	DEBIT	CREDIT	BALANCE DEBIT	BALANCE CREDIT

ACCOUNT _____ ACCOUNT NO. _____

DATE	ITEM	POST. REF.	DEBIT	CREDIT	BALANCE DEBIT	BALANCE CREDIT

e. _____

EXERCISE 2-9

a.

	JOURNAL				PAGE	

	DATE		DESCRIPTION	POST. REF.	DEBIT	CREDIT	
1							1
2							2
3							3
4							4
5							5
6							6
7							7
8							8
9							9
10							10
11							11

b.

Cash

Accounts Payable

Supplies

Fees Earned

Accounts Receivable

c. _____

_____

_____

_____

_____

EXERCISE 2-10

a. _____

_____

_____

_____

b. _____

_____

_____

EXERCISE 2-11

a.

Accounts Payable

b.

Accounts Receivable

c.

Cash

EXERCISE 2-12

a. _____

_____

_____

b. _____

_____

_____

EXERCISE 2-13

a. and b.

Transaction	Account Debited		Account Credited	
	Type	Effect	Type	Effect
(1)	asset	+	owner's equity	+
(2)				
(3)				
(4)				
(5)				
(6)				
(7)				
(8)				
(9)				

EXERCISE 2-14

	DATE		DESCRIPTION	POST. REF.	DEBIT	CREDIT	
1							1
2							2
3							3
4							4
5							5
6							6
7							7
8							8
9							9
10							10
11							11
12							12
13							13
14							14
15							15
16							16
17							17
18							18
19							19
20							20
21							21
22							22
23							23
24							24
25							25
26							26
27							27
28							28
29							29
30							30
31							31
32							32

JOURNAL PAGE

EXERCISE 2-15

a.

	Unadjusted Trial Balance		

b. _____

EXERCISE 2-16

Unadjusted Trial Balance		

EXERCISE 2-17

EXERCISE 2-18

Unadjusted Trial Balance		

EXERCISE 2-19

Error	(a) Out of Balance	(b) Difference	(c) Larger Total
1.	yes	$7,150	debit
2.			
3.			
4.			
5.			
6.			
7.			

EXERCISE 2-20

_____

_____

_____

_____

_____

_____

_____

_____

(Optional)

_____

Unadjusted Trial Balance

_____

EXERCISE 2-21

JOURNAL   PAGE

	DATE	DESCRIPTION	POST. REF.	DEBIT	CREDIT	
1						1
2						2
3						3
4						4
5						5

EXERCISE 2-22

JOURNAL   PAGE

	DATE		DESCRIPTION	POST. REF.	DEBIT	CREDIT	
1							1
2							2
3							3
4							4
5							5
6							6
7							7
8							8
9							9

EXERCISE 2-23

a. 1. Net sales: _____

_____

    2. Total operating expenses: _____

_____

b. _____

_____

_____

_____

_____

EXERCISE 2-24

a.

	Income Statement			
			Increase (Decrease)	
	2000	**1999**	**Amount**	**Percent**

b. _____

_____

_____

_____

_____

_____

_____

_____

_____

_____

_____

PROBLEM 2-1 ___

1. and 2.

Cash

Accounts Receivable

Supplies

Prepaid Insurance

Automobiles

PROBLEM 2-1 ___ , Continued

Equipment

Notes Payable

Accounts Payable

_____ , *Capital*

Professional Fees

Rent Expense

Salary Expense

PROBLEM 2-1 ___, Continued

Blueprint Expense

_____ | _____
_____ | _____
_____ | _____

Automobile Expense

_____ | _____
_____ | _____
_____ | _____

Miscellaneous Expense

_____ | _____
_____ | _____
_____ | _____
_____ | _____
_____ | _____

PROBLEM 2-1 ___ , Concluded

3.

	Unadjusted Trial Balance		

4. _____

PROBLEM 2-2 ___

1.

		JOURNAL			PAGE	

	DATE	DESCRIPTION	POST. REF.	DEBIT	CREDIT	
1						1
2						2
3						3
4						4
5						5
6						6
7						7
8						8
9						9
10						10
11						11
12						12
13						13
14						14
15						15
16						16
17						17
18						18
19						19
20						20
21						21
22						22
23						23
24						24
25						25
26						26
27						27
28						28
29						29
30						30
31						31
32						32
33						33
34						34
35						35
36						36

PROBLEM 2-2 ___, Continued

2.

Cash

_____ | _____

Supplies

_____ | _____

Accounts Payable

_____ | _____

_____, *Capital*

_____ | _____

_____, *Drawing*

_____ | _____

Sales Commissions

_____ | _____

PROBLEM 2-2 ___, Continued

Rent Expense

_____ | _____
_____ | _____
_____ | _____
_____ | _____

Office Salaries Expense

_____ | _____
_____ | _____
_____ | _____

Automobile Expense

_____ | _____
_____ | _____
_____ | _____

Supplies Expense

_____ | _____
_____ | _____
_____ | _____

Miscellaneous Expense

_____ | _____
_____ | _____
_____ | _____
_____ | _____

PROBLEM 2-2 ___ , Concluded

3.

Unadjusted Trial Balance		

4. a. _____

   b. _____

   c. _____

5. _____

PROBLEM 2-3 ___

1.

	JOURNAL				PAGE 1

	DATE	DESCRIPTION	POST. REF.	DEBIT	CREDIT	
1						1
2						2
3						3
4						4
5						5
6						6
7						7
8						8
9						9
10						10
11						11
12						12
13						13
14						14
15						15
16						16
17						17
18						18
19						19
20						20
21						21
22						22
23						23
24						24
25						25
26						26
27						27
28						28
29						29
30						30
31						31
32						32
33						33
34						34
35						35
36						36

PROBLEM 2-3 ___ , Continued

JOURNAL

PAGE 2

	DATE		DESCRIPTION	POST. REF.	DEBIT	CREDIT	
1							1
2							2
3							3
4							4
5							5
6							6
7							7
8							8
9							9
10							10
11							11
12							12
13							13
14							14
15							15
16							16
17							17
18							18
19							19
20							20
21							21
22							22
23							23
24							24
25							25
26							26
27							27
28							28
29							29
30							30
31							31
32							32
33							33
34							34
35							35
36							36

PROBLEM 2-3 ___, Continued

2.

GENERAL LEDGER

ACCOUNT   *Cash*   ACCOUNT NO.   11

DATE	ITEM	POST. REF.	DEBIT	CREDIT	BALANCE DEBIT	BALANCE CREDIT

ACCOUNT   *Accounts Receivable*   ACCOUNT NO.   12

DATE	ITEM	POST. REF.	DEBIT	CREDIT	BALANCE DEBIT	BALANCE CREDIT

ACCOUNT   *Supplies*   ACCOUNT NO.   13

DATE	ITEM	POST. REF.	DEBIT	CREDIT	BALANCE DEBIT	BALANCE CREDIT

PROBLEM 2-3 ___ , Continued

ACCOUNT   *Prepaid Insurance*   ACCOUNT NO.   14

DATE		ITEM	POST. REF.	DEBIT	CREDIT	BALANCE	
						DEBIT	CREDIT

ACCOUNT   *Equipment*   ACCOUNT NO.   16

DATE		ITEM	POST. REF.	DEBIT	CREDIT	BALANCE	
						DEBIT	CREDIT

ACCOUNT   *Truck*   ACCOUNT NO.   18

DATE		ITEM	POST. REF.	DEBIT	CREDIT	BALANCE	
						DEBIT	CREDIT

ACCOUNT   *Notes Payable*   ACCOUNT NO.   21

DATE		ITEM	POST. REF.	DEBIT	CREDIT	BALANCE	
						DEBIT	CREDIT

ACCOUNT   *Accounts Payable*   ACCOUNT NO.   22

DATE		ITEM	POST. REF.	DEBIT	CREDIT	BALANCE	
						DEBIT	CREDIT

PROBLEM 2-3 ___ , Continued

ACCOUNT _____, *Capital*   ACCOUNT NO.   *31*

DATE		ITEM	POST. REF.	DEBIT	CREDIT	BALANCE	
						DEBIT	CREDIT

ACCOUNT _____, *Drawing*   ACCOUNT NO.   *32*

DATE		ITEM	POST. REF.	DEBIT	CREDIT	BALANCE	
						DEBIT	CREDIT

ACCOUNT   *Fees Earned*   ACCOUNT NO.   *41*

DATE		ITEM	POST. REF.	DEBIT	CREDIT	BALANCE	
						DEBIT	CREDIT

PROBLEM 2-3 ___, Continued

ACCOUNT   *Wages Expense*   ACCOUNT NO.   *51*

DATE		ITEM	POST. REF.	DEBIT	CREDIT	BALANCE	
						DEBIT	CREDIT

ACCOUNT   *Rent Expense*   ACCOUNT NO.   *53*

DATE		ITEM	POST. REF.	DEBIT	CREDIT	BALANCE	
						DEBIT	CREDIT

ACCOUNT   *Utilities Expense*   ACCOUNT NO.   *54*

DATE		ITEM	POST. REF.	DEBIT	CREDIT	BALANCE	
						DEBIT	CREDIT

ACCOUNT   *Truck Expense*   ACCOUNT NO.   *55*

DATE		ITEM	POST. REF.	DEBIT	CREDIT	BALANCE	
						DEBIT	CREDIT

ACCOUNT   *Miscellaneous Expense*   ACCOUNT NO.   *59*

DATE		ITEM	POST. REF.	DEBIT	CREDIT	BALANCE	
						DEBIT	CREDIT

PROBLEM 2-3 ___ , Concluded

3.

		Unadjusted Trial Balance				

4. _____

5. _____

_____

_____

This Page Not Used.

PROBLEM 2-4 ___

2. and 3.

JOURNAL

PAGE *18*

	DATE		DESCRIPTION	POST. REF.	DEBIT	CREDIT	
1							1
2							2
3							3
4							4
5							5
6							6
7							7
8							8
9							9
10							10
11							11
12							12
13							13
14							14
15							15
16							16
17							17
18							18
19							19
20							20
21							21
22							22
23							23
24							24
25							25
26							26
27							27
28							28
29							29
30							30
31							31
32							32
33							33
34							34
35							35
36							36

PROBLEM 2-4 ___, Continued

JOURNAL   PAGE *19*

	DATE		DESCRIPTION	POST. REF.	DEBIT	CREDIT	
1							1
2							2
3							3
4							4
5							5
6							6
7							7
8							8
9							9
10							10
11							11
12							12
13							13
14							14
15							15
16							16
17							17
18							18
19							19
20							20
21							21
22							22
23							23
24							24
25							25
26							26
27							27
28							28
29							29
30							30
31							31
32							32
33							33
34							34
35							35
36							36

PROBLEM 2-4 ___ , Continued

1. and 3.

ACCOUNT   *Cash*   ACCOUNT NO.   11

DATE		ITEM	POST. REF.	DEBIT	CREDIT	BALANCE	
						DEBIT	CREDIT

ACCOUNT   *Accounts Receivable*   ACCOUNT NO.   12

DATE		ITEM	POST. REF.	DEBIT	CREDIT	BALANCE	
						DEBIT	CREDIT

ACCOUNT   *Prepaid Insurance*   ACCOUNT NO.   13

DATE		ITEM	POST. REF.	DEBIT	CREDIT	BALANCE	
						DEBIT	CREDIT

PROBLEM 2-4 ___, Continued

ACCOUNT   *Office Supplies*   ACCOUNT NO.   14

DATE		ITEM	POST. REF.	DEBIT	CREDIT	BALANCE	
						DEBIT	CREDIT

ACCOUNT   *Land*   ACCOUNT NO.   16

DATE		ITEM	POST. REF.	DEBIT	CREDIT	BALANCE	
						DEBIT	CREDIT

ACCOUNT   *Accounts Payable*   ACCOUNT NO.   21

DATE		ITEM	POST. REF.	DEBIT	CREDIT	BALANCE	
						DEBIT	CREDIT

ACCOUNT   *Unearned Rent*   ACCOUNT NO.   22

DATE		ITEM	POST. REF.	DEBIT	CREDIT	BALANCE	
						DEBIT	CREDIT

ACCOUNT   *Notes Payable*   ACCOUNT NO.   23

DATE		ITEM	POST. REF.	DEBIT	CREDIT	BALANCE	
						DEBIT	CREDIT

PROBLEM 2-4 ___, Continued

ACCOUNT _____, *Capital*   ACCOUNT NO.   31

DATE	ITEM	POST. REF.	DEBIT	CREDIT	BALANCE DEBIT	CREDIT

ACCOUNT _____, *Drawing*   ACCOUNT NO.   32

DATE	ITEM	POST. REF.	DEBIT	CREDIT	BALANCE DEBIT	CREDIT

ACCOUNT   *Fees Earned*   ACCOUNT NO.   41

DATE	ITEM	POST. REF.	DEBIT	CREDIT	BALANCE DEBIT	CREDIT

ACCOUNT   *Salary and Commission Expense*   ACCOUNT NO.   51

DATE	ITEM	POST. REF.	DEBIT	CREDIT	BALANCE DEBIT	CREDIT

PROBLEM 2-4 ___ , Continued

ACCOUNT   *Rent Expense*   ACCOUNT NO.   *52*

DATE		ITEM	POST. REF.	DEBIT	CREDIT	BALANCE	
						DEBIT	CREDIT

ACCOUNT   *Advertising Expense*   ACCOUNT NO.   *53*

DATE		ITEM	POST. REF.	DEBIT	CREDIT	BALANCE	
						DEBIT	CREDIT

ACCOUNT   *Automobile Expense*   ACCOUNT NO.   *54*

DATE		ITEM	POST. REF.	DEBIT	CREDIT	BALANCE	
						DEBIT	CREDIT

ACCOUNT   *Miscellaneous Expense*   ACCOUNT NO.   *59*

DATE		ITEM	POST. REF.	DEBIT	CREDIT	BALANCE	
						DEBIT	CREDIT

PROBLEM 2-4 ___, Concluded

4.

_____

Unadjusted Trial Balance

_____

5. a. _____

_____

_____

b. Journal entry:

JOURNAL

PAGE

	DATE		DESCRIPTION	POST. REF.	DEBIT	CREDIT	
1							1
2							2
3							3
4							4
5							5
6							6

c. _____

This Page Not Used.

PROBLEM 2-5 ___

JOURNAL   PAGE *19*

	DATE		DESCRIPTION	POST. REF.	DEBIT	CREDIT	
1	20— May	1	Rent Expense	52	1,540.00		1
2			Cash	11		1,540.00	2
3							3
4		4	Supplies	12	149.00		4
5			Accounts Payable	22		149.00	5
6							6
7		6	Advertising Expense	54	275.00		7
8			Cash	11		275.00	8
9							9
10		8	Cash	11	1,595.30		10
11			Service Revenue	41		1,595.30	11
12							12
13		9	Prepaid Insurance	13	144.00		13
14			Cash	11		144.00	14
15							15
16		10	Land	16	12,000.00		16
17			Cash	11		5,500.00	17
18			Notes Payable	21		6,500.00	18
19							19
20		13	Accounts Payable	22	847.20		20
21			Cash	11		847.20	21
22							22
23		14	Miscellaneous Expense	58	162.10		23
24			Cash	11		162.10	24
25							25
26		15	Wages Expense	51	1,128.60		26
27			Cash	11		1,128.60	27
28							28
29		15	Cash	11	1,785.50		29
30			Service Revenue	41		1,785.50	30
31							31
32		16	Diann Adler, Drawing	32	750.00		32
33			Cash	11		750.00	33
34							34
35		17	Supplies	12	212.60		35
36			Accounts Payable	22		212.60	36

PROBLEM 2-5 ___ , Continued

JOURNAL

	DATE		DESCRIPTION	POST. REF.	DEBIT	CREDIT	
1	20— May	20	Cash	11	1,662.20		1
2			Service Revenue	41		1,662.20	2
3							3
4		22	Accounts Payable	22	74.20		4
5			Supplies	12		74.20	5
6							6
7		25	Miscellaneous Expense	58	121.40		7
8			Cash	11		121.40	8
9							9
10		25	Cash	11	1,681.30		10
11			Service Revenue	41		1,681.30	11
12							12
13		30	Utilities Expense	53	436.60		13
14			Cash	11		436.60	14
15							15
16		31	Wages Expense	51	1,390.00		16
17			Cash	11		1,390.00	17
18							18
19		31	Diann Adler, Drawing	32	600.00		19
20			Cash	11		600.00	20
21							21
22		31	Cash	11	1,276.10		22
23			Service Revenue	41		1,276.10	23
24							24
25							25
26							26
27							27
28							28
29							29
30							30
31							31
32							32
33							33
34							34
35							35
36							36

PROBLEM 2-5 ___, Continued

1. and 3.

ACCOUNT   *Cash*   ACCOUNT NO.   *11*

DATE		ITEM	POST. REF.	DEBIT	CREDIT	BALANCE	
						DEBIT	CREDIT
20— May	1	Balance	√			13,810.50	
	1		19		1,540.00		
	6		19		275.00		
	8		19	1,595.30			
	9		19		144.00		
	10		19		5,500.00		
	13		19		847.20		
	14		19		162.10		
	15		19		1,128.60		
	15		19	1,785.50			
	16		19		750.00		
	20		20	1,662.20			
	25		20		121.40		
	25		20	1,681.30			
	30		20		346.60		
	31		20		1,390.00		
	31		20		600.00		
	31		20	1,276.10		9,006.00	

ACCOUNT   *Supplies*   ACCOUNT NO.   *12*

DATE		ITEM	POST. REF.	DEBIT	CREDIT	BALANCE	
						DEBIT	CREDIT
20— May	1	Balance	√			710.50	
	4		19	149.00			
	17		19	212.60			
	22		20		74.20	997.90	

ACCOUNT   *Prepaid Insurance*   ACCOUNT NO.   *13*

DATE		ITEM	POST. REF.	DEBIT	CREDIT	BALANCE	
						DEBIT	CREDIT
20— May	1	Balance	√			251.50	
	9		19	14.40		265.90	

PROBLEM 2-5 ___, Continued

ACCOUNT   *Land*   ACCOUNT NO.   16

DATE		ITEM	POST. REF.	DEBIT	CREDIT	BALANCE DEBIT	BALANCE CREDIT
20— May	1	Balance	√	14,625.00		14,625.00	
	10		19	1,200.00		15,825.00	

ACCOUNT   *Notes Payable*   ACCOUNT NO.   21

DATE		ITEM	POST. REF.	DEBIT	CREDIT	BALANCE DEBIT	BALANCE CREDIT
20— May	10		19		6,500.00		6,500.00

ACCOUNT   *Accounts Payable*   ACCOUNT NO.   22

DATE		ITEM	POST. REF.	DEBIT	CREDIT	BALANCE DEBIT	BALANCE CREDIT
20— May	1	Balance	√				1,637.30
	4		19		149.00		
	13		19	847.20			
	17		19		212.60		
	22		20	74.20			1,151.70

ACCOUNT   *Diann Adler, Capital*   ACCOUNT NO.   31

DATE		ITEM	POST. REF.	DEBIT	CREDIT	BALANCE DEBIT	BALANCE CREDIT
20— May	1	Balance	√				27,760.20

PROBLEM 2-5 ___, Continued

ACCOUNT   *Diann Adler, Drawing*   ACCOUNT NO.   32

DATE		ITEM	POST. REF.	DEBIT	CREDIT	BALANCE DEBIT	BALANCE CREDIT
20— May	16		19	750.00			
	31		20	600.00		1,350.00	

ACCOUNT   *Service Revenue*   ACCOUNT NO.   41

DATE		ITEM	POST. REF.	DEBIT	CREDIT	BALANCE DEBIT	BALANCE CREDIT
20— May	8		19		1,595.30		
	15		19		1,785.50		
	20		20		1,662.20		
	25		20		1,681.30		
	31		20		1,276.10		8,000.40

ACCOUNT   *Wages Expense*   ACCOUNT NO.   51

DATE		ITEM	POST. REF.	DEBIT	CREDIT	BALANCE DEBIT	BALANCE CREDIT
20— May	15		19	1,128.60			
	31		20	1,930.00		3,058.60	

PROBLEM 2-5 ___, Continued

ACCOUNT   *Rent Expense*   ACCOUNT NO.   52

DATE		ITEM	POST. REF.	DEBIT	CREDIT	BALANCE	
						DEBIT	CREDIT
20— May	1		19	1,540.00		1,540.00	

ACCOUNT   *Utilities Expense*   ACCOUNT NO.   53

DATE		ITEM	POST. REF.	DEBIT	CREDIT	BALANCE	
						DEBIT	CREDIT
20— May	30		20	436.60		436.60	

ACCOUNT   *Advertising Expense*   ACCOUNT NO.   54

DATE		ITEM	POST. REF.	DEBIT	CREDIT	BALANCE	
						DEBIT	CREDIT
20— May	6		19	275.00		275.00	

ACCOUNT   *Miscellaneous Expense*   ACCOUNT NO.   58

DATE		ITEM	POST. REF.	DEBIT	CREDIT	BALANCE	
						DEBIT	CREDIT
20— May	14		19	162.10		162.10	
	25		20	121.40		283.50	

PROBLEM 2-5 ___ , Continued

A-AALL ELECTRONIC REPAIR
Unadjusted Trial Balance
May 31, 20—

Cash	9,006.00	
Supplies	979.90	
Prepaid Insurance	265.90	
Land	15,825.00	
Notes Payable		650.00
Accounts Payable		1,151.70
Diann Adler, Capital		27,760.20
Diann Adler, Drawing		1,350.00
Service Revenue		8,000.40
Wages Expense	3,058.60	
Utilities Expense	436.60	
Advertising Expense	275.00	
Miscellaneous Expense	283.50	
	30,130.50	38,912.30

PROBLEM 2-5 ___, Continued

Verification Schedule

1. Totals of preliminary trial balance: Debit $ _____

                                             Credit $ _____

2. Difference between preliminary trial balance totals: $ _____

3. Errors in trial balance:

_____

_____

_____

_____

_____

_____

4. Errors in account balances:

_____

_____

5. Errors in posting:

_____

_____

_____

_____

_____

_____

_____

_____

_____

6. Journal entry:

JOURNAL   PAGE *19*

	DATE		DESCRIPTION	POST. REF.	DEBIT	CREDIT	
1							1
2							2
3							3
4							4

PROBLEM 2-5 ___, Concluded

7.

	A_AALL ELECTRONIC REPAIR		
	Unadjusted Trial Balance		
	May 31, 20—		

84

This Page Not Used.

PROBLEM 2-6 ___

1.

			Debit Balances	Credit Balances
Cash				
Accounts Receivable				
Supplies				
Prepaid Insurance				
Equipment				
Notes Payable				
Accounts Payable				
_____, Capital				
_____, Drawing				
Fees Earned				
Wages Expense				
Rent Expense				
Advertising Expense				
Gas, Electricity, and Water Expense				
Miscellaneous Expense				

Corrected Unadjusted Trial Balance

2.

_____

_____

_____

_____

_____

_____

_____

_____

_____

_____

_____

This Page Not Used.

CONTINUING PROBLEM

2. and 3.

JOURNAL PAGE *1*

	DATE	DESCRIPTION	POST. REF.	DEBIT	CREDIT	
1						1
2						2
3						3
4						4
5						5
6						6
7						7
8						8
9						9
10						10
11						11
12						12
13						13
14						14
15						15
16						16
17						17
18						18
19						19
20						20
21						21
22						22
23						23
24						24
25						25
26						26
27						27
28						28
29						29
30						30
31						31
32						32
33						33
34						34
35						35
36						36

CONTINUING PROBLEM, Continued

2. and 3.

JOURNAL

	DATE		DESCRIPTION	POST. REF.	DEBIT	CREDIT	
1							1
2							2
3							3
4							4
5							5
6							6
7							7
8							8
9							9
10							10
11							11
12							12
13							13
14							14
15							15
16							16
17							17
18							18
19							19
20							20
21							21
22							22
23							23
24							24
25							25
26							26
27							27
28							28
29							29
30							30
31							31
32							32
33							33
34							34
35							35
36							36

CONTINUING PROBLEM, Continued

1. and 3.

GENERAL LEDGER

ACCOUNT *Cash* ACCOUNT NO. *11*

DATE		ITEM	POST. REF.	DEBIT	CREDIT	BALANCE	
						DEBIT	CREDIT

ACCOUNT *Accounts Receivable* ACCOUNT NO. *12*

DATE		ITEM	POST. REF.	DEBIT	CREDIT	BALANCE	
						DEBIT	CREDIT

CONTINUING PROBLEM, Continued

ACCOUNT   *Supplies*   ACCOUNT NO.   14

DATE		ITEM	POST. REF.	DEBIT	CREDIT	BALANCE	
						DEBIT	CREDIT

ACCOUNT   *Prepaid Insurance*   ACCOUNT NO.   15

DATE		ITEM	POST. REF.	DEBIT	CREDIT	BALANCE	
						DEBIT	CREDIT

ACCOUNT   *Office Equipment*   ACCOUNT NO.   17

DATE		ITEM	POST. REF.	DEBIT	CREDIT	BALANCE	
						DEBIT	CREDIT

ACCOUNT   *Accumulated Depreciation—Office Equipment*   ACCOUNT NO.   18

DATE		ITEM	POST. REF.	DEBIT	CREDIT	BALANCE	
						DEBIT	CREDIT

(This account is not used in Chapter 2.)

ACCOUNT   *Accounts Payable*   ACCOUNT NO.   21

DATE		ITEM	POST. REF.	DEBIT	CREDIT	BALANCE	
						DEBIT	CREDIT

CONTINUING PROBLEM, Continued

ACCOUNT *Wages Payable* ACCOUNT NO. 22

DATE	ITEM	POST. REF.	DEBIT	CREDIT	BALANCE DEBIT	BALANCE CREDIT

(This account is not used in Chapter 2.)

ACCOUNT *Unearned Revenue* ACCOUNT NO. 23

DATE	ITEM	POST. REF.	DEBIT	CREDIT	BALANCE DEBIT	BALANCE CREDIT

ACCOUNT *Pat Sharpe, Capital* ACCOUNT NO. 31

DATE	ITEM	POST. REF.	DEBIT	CREDIT	BALANCE DEBIT	BALANCE CREDIT

ACCOUNT *Pat Sharpe, Drawing* ACCOUNT NO. 32

DATE	ITEM	POST. REF.	DEBIT	CREDIT	BALANCE DEBIT	BALANCE CREDIT

ACCOUNT *Income Summary* ACCOUNT NO. 33

DATE	ITEM	POST. REF.	DEBIT	CREDIT	BALANCE DEBIT	BALANCE CREDIT

(This account is not used in Chapter 2.)

CONTINUING PROBLEM, Continued

ACCOUNT *Fees Earned*   ACCOUNT NO. *41*

DATE		ITEM	POST. REF.	DEBIT	CREDIT	BALANCE	
						DEBIT	CREDIT

ACCOUNT *Wages Expense*   ACCOUNT NO. *50*

DATE		ITEM	POST. REF.	DEBIT	CREDIT	BALANCE	
						DEBIT	CREDIT

ACCOUNT *Office Rent Expense*   ACCOUNT NO. *51*

DATE		ITEM	POST. REF.	DEBIT	CREDIT	BALANCE	
						DEBIT	CREDIT

ACCOUNT *Equipment Rent Expense*   ACCOUNT NO. *52*

DATE		ITEM	POST. REF.	DEBIT	CREDIT	BALANCE	
						DEBIT	CREDIT

CONTINUING PROBLEM, Continued

ACCOUNT *Utilities Expense*   ACCOUNT NO. 53

DATE		ITEM	POST. REF.	DEBIT	CREDIT	BALANCE	
						DEBIT	CREDIT

ACCOUNT *Music Expense*   ACCOUNT NO. 54

DATE		ITEM	POST. REF.	DEBIT	CREDIT	BALANCE	
						DEBIT	CREDIT

ACCOUNT *Advertising Expense*   ACCOUNT NO. 55

DATE		ITEM	POST. REF.	DEBIT	CREDIT	BALANCE	
						DEBIT	CREDIT

ACCOUNT *Supplies Expense*   ACCOUNT NO. 56

DATE		ITEM	POST. REF.	DEBIT	CREDIT	BALANCE	
						DEBIT	CREDIT

ACCOUNT *Insurance Expense*   ACCOUNT NO. 57

DATE		ITEM	POST. REF.	DEBIT	CREDIT	BALANCE	
						DEBIT	CREDIT

(This account is not used in Chapter 2.)

CONTINUING PROBLEM, Concluded

ACCOUNT   *Depreciation Expense*   ACCOUNT NO.   *58*

DATE	ITEM	POST. REF.	DEBIT	CREDIT	BALANCE DEBIT	BALANCE CREDIT

(This account is not used in Chapter 2.)

ACCOUNT   *Miscellaneous Expense*   ACCOUNT NO.   *59*

DATE	ITEM	POST. REF.	DEBIT	CREDIT	BALANCE DEBIT	BALANCE CREDIT

4.

Unadjusted Trial Balance

EXERCISE 3-1

1. A three-year premium paid on a fire insurance policy: _____

2. Fees earned but not yet received: _____

3. Fees received but not yet earned: _____

4. Salary owed but not yet paid: _____

5. Subscriptions received in advance by a magazine publisher: _____

6. Supplies on hand: _____

7. Taxes owed but payable in the following period: _____

8. Utilities owed but not yet paid: _____

EXERCISE 3-2

Account	Answer
Accounts Receivable	Normally requires adjustment (AR). _____
Cash.........................	_____
Interest Expense......................	_____
Interest Receivable...................	_____
Johann Atkins, Capital..............	_____
Land.........................	_____
Office Equipment	_____
Prepaid Rent...........................	_____
Supplies	_____
Unearned Fees........................	_____
Wages Expense.......................	_____

EXERCISE 3-3

JOURNAL

PAGE

	DATE	DESCRIPTION	POST. REF.	DEBIT	CREDIT	
1						1
2						2
3						3

EXERCISE 3-4

_____

_____

EXERCISE 3-5

a. _____

_____

_____

b. _____

_____

_____

EXERCISE 3-6

a. and b.

JOURNAL   PAGE _____

	DATE		DESCRIPTION	POST. REF.	DEBIT	CREDIT	
1							1
2							2
3							3
4							4
5							5
6							6

EXERCISE 3-7

a. and b.

JOURNAL   PAGE _____

	DATE		DESCRIPTION	POST. REF.	DEBIT	CREDIT	
1							1
2							2
3							3
4							4
5							5
6							6

EXERCISE 3-8

JOURNAL   PAGE _____

	DATE		DESCRIPTION	POST. REF.	DEBIT	CREDIT	
1							1
2							2
3							3

EXERCISE 3-9

a. _____
   _____
   _____

b. _____
   _____
   _____

EXERCISE 3-10

a.

JOURNAL   PAGE

	DATE		DESCRIPTION	POST. REF.	DEBIT	CREDIT	
1							1
2							2
3							3

b.

   _____
   _____
   _____
   _____

EXERCISE 3-11

a. and b.

JOURNAL   PAGE

	DATE		DESCRIPTION	POST. REF.	DEBIT	CREDIT	
1							1
2							2
3							3
4							4
5							5
6							6
7							7

EXERCISE 3-12

a. _____

_____

b. _____

_____

EXERCISE 3-13

a. and b.

JOURNAL   PAGE

	DATE		DESCRIPTION	POST. REF.	DEBIT	CREDIT	
1							1
2							2
3							3
4							4
5							5
6							6
7							7

EXERCISE 3-14

_____

_____

_____

EXERCISE 3-15

a. _____

_____

_____

_____

b. _____

_____

_____

_____

EXERCISE 3-16

a. _____

_____

b. _____

_____

_____

EXERCISE 3-17

a.

JOURNAL PAGE

	DATE		DESCRIPTION	POST. REF.	DEBIT	CREDIT	
1							1
2							2
3							3
4							4
5							5
6							6
7							7

b. _____

EXERCISE 3-18

JOURNAL PAGE

	DATE		DESCRIPTION	POST. REF.	DEBIT	CREDIT	
1							1
2							2
3							3
4							4
5							5

EXERCISE 3-19

a. _____

b. _____

_____

_____

EXERCISE 3-20

a. _____

b. _____

_____

_____

_____

_____

EXERCISE 3-21

_____

EXERCISE 3-22

a. _____

b. _____

EXERCISE 3-23

	Error (a)		Error (b)	
	Overstated	Understated	Overstated	Understated
1. Revenue for the year would be	$	$	$	$
2. Expenses for the year would be	$	$	$	$
3. Net income for the year would be	$	$	$	$
4. Assets at May 31 would be	$	$	$	$
5. Liabilities at May 31 would be	$	$	$	$
6. Owner's equity at May 31 would be	$	$	$	$

EXERCISE 3-24

_____

_____

EXERCISE 3-25

a.

JOURNAL

PAGE

	DATE		DESCRIPTION	POST. REF.	DEBIT	CREDIT	
1							1
2							2
3							3

EXERCISE 3-25, Concluded

b. **(1)** _____

_____

_____

(2) _____

_____

_____

EXERCISE 3-26

JOURNAL   PAGE

	DATE		DESCRIPTION	POST. REF.	DEBIT	CREDIT	
1							1
2							2
3							3
4							4
5							5
6							6
7							7
8							8
9							9
10							10
11							11
12							12
13							13
14							14

EXERCISE 3-27

EXERCISE 3-27, Concluded
(Optional)

Adjusted Trial Balance		

EXERCISE 3-28

a. _____

_____

b. _____

_____

c. _____

_____

_____

_____

EXERCISE 3-29

a. Dell Inc.

	Amount	Percent

b. Hewlett-Packard Company (HP)

	Amount	Percent

c. _____

_____

_____

_____

_____

_____

_____

_____

_____

PROBLEM 3-1 ___

1.

JOURNAL

PAGE

	DATE		DESCRIPTION	POST. REF.	DEBIT	CREDIT	
1							1
2							2
3							3
4							4
5							5
6							6
7							7
8							8
9							9
10							10
11							11
12							12
13							13
14							14
15							15
16							16
17							17
18							18
19							19
20							20

2.

_____

_____

_____

This Page Not Used.

PROBLEM 3-2 ___

1.   **JOURNAL**   PAGE

	DATE		DESCRIPTION	POST. REF.	DEBIT	CREDIT	
1							1
2							2
3							3
4							4
5							5
6							6
7							7
8							8
9							9
10							10
11							11
12							12
13							13
14							14
15							15
16							16
17							17
18							18
19							19
20							20
21							21
22							22
23							23
24							24
25							25
26							26
27							27
28							28
29							29
30							30
31							31
32							32
33							33
34							34
35							35
36							36

PROBLEM 3-2 ___, Concluded

2.

_____

_____

_____

3.

_____

_____

_____

_____

_____

4.

_____

_____

_____

PROBLEM 3-3 ___

1.

JOURNAL

PAGE

	DATE		DESCRIPTION	POST. REF.	DEBIT	CREDIT	
1							1
2							2
3							3
4							4
5							5
6							6
7							7
8							8
9							9
10							10
11							11
12							12
13							13
14							14
15							15
16							16
17							17
18							18
19							19
20							20
21							21
22							22
23							23
24							24
25							25
26							26
27							27
28							28
29							29
30							30
31							31
32							32
33							33
34							34
35							35
36							36

PROBLEM 3-3 ___, Concluded

2.

	Amount

3.

	Amount

4.

_____

_____

_____

PROBLEM 3-4 ___

JOURNAL   PAGE

	DATE	DESCRIPTION	POST. REF.	DEBIT	CREDIT	
1						1
2						2
3						3
4						4
5						5
6						6
7						7
8						8
9						9
10						10
11						11
12						12
13						13
14						14
15						15
16						16
17						17
18						18
19						19
20						20
21						21
22						22
23						23
24						24
25						25
26						26
27						27
28						28
29						29
30						30
31						31
32						32
33						33
34						34
35						35
36						36

This Page Not Used.

PROBLEM 3-5 ___

1.

	JOURNAL				PAGE	
DATE	DESCRIPTION	POST. REF.	DEBIT	CREDIT		
1						1
2						2
3						3
4						4
5						5
6						6
7						7
8						8
9						9
10						10
11						11
12						12
13						13
14						14
15						15
16						16
17						17
18						18
19						19
20						20
21						21
22						22
23						23
24						24
25						25
26						26
27						27
28						28
29						29
30						30
31						31
32						32
33						33
34						34
35						35
36						36

PROBLEM 3-5 ___, Concluded

2.

Adjusted Trial Balance		

PROBLEM 3-6 ___

1.

	JOURNAL			PAGE

	DATE		DESCRIPTION	POST. REF.	DEBIT	CREDIT	
1							1
2							2
3							3
4							4
5							5
6							6
7							7
8							8
9							9
10							10
11							11
12							12
13							13
14							14
15							15
16							16
17							17
18							18
19							19
20							20
21							21
22							22
23							23
24							24
25							25
26							26
27							27
28							28
29							29
30							30
31							31
32							32
33							33
34							34
35							35
36							36

PROBLEM 3-6 ___ , Concluded

2.

	Net Income	Total Assets	=	Total Liabilities	+	Total Owner's Equity
Reported amounts	$	$		$		$
Corrections:						
Adjustment (a)						
Adjustment (b)						
Adjustment (c)						
Adjustment (d)						
Corrected amounts	$	$		$		$

CONTINUING PROBLEM

1.

JOURNAL   PAGE 3

	DATE	DESCRIPTION	POST. REF.	DEBIT	CREDIT	
1						1
2						2
3						3
4						4
5						5
6						6
7						7
8						8
9						9
10						10
11						11
12						12
13						13
14						14
15						15
16						16
17						17
18						18
19						19
20						20
21						21
22						22
23						23
24						24
25						25
26						26
27						27
28						28
29						29
30						30
31						31
32						32
33						33
34						34
35						35
36						36

CONTINUING PROBLEM, Continued

2.

ACCOUNT   *Cash*   ACCOUNT NO.   *11*

DATE	ITEM	POST. REF.	DEBIT	CREDIT	BALANCE	
					DEBIT	CREDIT

ACCOUNT   *Accounts Receivable*   ACCOUNT NO.   *12*

DATE	ITEM	POST. REF.	DEBIT	CREDIT	BALANCE	
					DEBIT	CREDIT

CONTINUING PROBLEM, Continued

ACCOUNT   *Supplies*   ACCOUNT NO.   14

DATE		ITEM	POST. REF.	DEBIT	CREDIT	BALANCE	
						DEBIT	CREDIT

ACCOUNT   *Prepaid Insurance*   ACCOUNT NO.   15

DATE		ITEM	POST. REF.	DEBIT	CREDIT	BALANCE	
						DEBIT	CREDIT

ACCOUNT   *Office Equipment*   ACCOUNT NO.   17

DATE		ITEM	POST. REF.	DEBIT	CREDIT	BALANCE	
						DEBIT	CREDIT

ACCOUNT   *Accumulated Depreciation—Office Equipment*   ACCOUNT NO.   18

DATE		ITEM	POST. REF.	DEBIT	CREDIT	BALANCE	
						DEBIT	CREDIT

ACCOUNT   *Accounts Payable*   ACCOUNT NO.   21

DATE		ITEM	POST. REF.	DEBIT	CREDIT	BALANCE	
						DEBIT	CREDIT

CONTINUING PROBLEM, Continued

ACCOUNT   *Wages Payable*   ACCOUNT NO. *22*

DATE		ITEM	POST. REF.	DEBIT	CREDIT	BALANCE DEBIT	BALANCE CREDIT

ACCOUNT   *Unearned Revenue*   ACCOUNT NO. *23*

DATE		ITEM	POST. REF.	DEBIT	CREDIT	BALANCE DEBIT	BALANCE CREDIT

ACCOUNT   *Pat Sharpe, Capital*   ACCOUNT NO. *31*

DATE		ITEM	POST. REF.	DEBIT	CREDIT	BALANCE DEBIT	BALANCE CREDIT

ACCOUNT   *Pat Sharpe, Drawing*   ACCOUNT NO. *32*

DATE		ITEM	POST. REF.	DEBIT	CREDIT	BALANCE DEBIT	BALANCE CREDIT

ACCOUNT   *Income Summary*   ACCOUNT NO. *33*

DATE		ITEM	POST. REF.	DEBIT	CREDIT	BALANCE DEBIT	BALANCE CREDIT

CONTINUING PROBLEM, Continued

ACCOUNT   *Fees Earned*   ACCOUNT NO.   *41*

DATE		ITEM	POST. REF.	DEBIT	CREDIT	BALANCE	
						DEBIT	CREDIT

ACCOUNT   *Wages Expense*   ACCOUNT NO.   *50*

DATE		ITEM	POST. REF.	DEBIT	CREDIT	BALANCE	
						DEBIT	CREDIT

ACCOUNT   *Office Rent Expense*   ACCOUNT NO.   *51*

DATE		ITEM	POST. REF.	DEBIT	CREDIT	BALANCE	
						DEBIT	CREDIT

ACCOUNT   *Equipment Rent Expense*   ACCOUNT NO.   *52*

DATE		ITEM	POST. REF.	DEBIT	CREDIT	BALANCE	
						DEBIT	CREDIT

CONTINUING PROBLEM, Continued

ACCOUNT *Utilities Expense*   ACCOUNT NO. 53

DATE	ITEM	POST. REF.	DEBIT	CREDIT	BALANCE DEBIT	CREDIT

ACCOUNT *Music Expense*   ACCOUNT NO. 54

DATE	ITEM	POST. REF.	DEBIT	CREDIT	BALANCE DEBIT	CREDIT

ACCOUNT *Advertising Expense*   ACCOUNT NO. 55

DATE	ITEM	POST. REF.	DEBIT	CREDIT	BALANCE DEBIT	CREDIT

ACCOUNT *Supplies Expense*   ACCOUNT NO. 56

DATE	ITEM	POST. REF.	DEBIT	CREDIT	BALANCE DEBIT	CREDIT

ACCOUNT *Insurance Expense*   ACCOUNT NO. 57

DATE	ITEM	POST. REF.	DEBIT	CREDIT	BALANCE DEBIT	CREDIT

CONTINUING PROBLEM, Continued

ACCOUNT   *Depreciation Expense*   ACCOUNT NO.   *58*

DATE		ITEM	POST. REF.	DEBIT	CREDIT	BALANCE	
						DEBIT	CREDIT

ACCOUNT   *Miscellaneous Expense*   ACCOUNT NO.   *59*

DATE		ITEM	POST. REF.	DEBIT	CREDIT	BALANCE	
						DEBIT	CREDIT

CONTINUING PROBLEM, Concluded

3.

	Adjusted Trial Balance	

EXERCISE 4-1

1. Accounts Payable: _____

2. Accounts Receivable: _____

3. Cash: _____

4. Dora Kovar, Drawing: _____

5. Fees Earned: _____

6. Supplies: _____

7. Unearned Rent: _____

8. Utilities Expense: _____

9. Wages Expense: _____

10. Wages Payable: _____

EXERCISE 4-2

1. Accounts Receivable: _____

2. Equipment: _____

3. Fees Earned: _____

4. Insurance Expense: _____

5. Prepaid Advertising: _____

6. Prepaid Insurance: _____

7. Rent Revenue: _____

8. Salary Expense: _____

9. Salary Payable: _____

10. Supplies: _____

11. Supplies Expense: _____

12. Unearned Rent: _____

EXERCISE 4-3

	Income Statement		

	Statement of Owner's Equity		

EXERCISE 4-3, Concluded

Balance Sheet

EXERCISE 4-4

Income Statement

Statement of Owner's Equity

EXERCISE 4-4, Concluded

Chapter 4

Balance Sheet

EXERCISE 4-5

		Income Statement			

EXERCISE 4-6

		Income Statement			

EXERCISE 4-7

a.

Income Statement		

b.

_____

_____

_____

_____

_____

_____

EXERCISE 4-8

Statement of Owner's Equity		

EXERCISE 4-9

Statement of Owner's Equity		

EXERCISE 4-10

1. Accounts receivable: _____

2. Building: _____

3. Cash: _____

4. Equipment: _____

5. Prepaid Insurance: _____

6. Supplies: _____

EXERCISE 4-11

_____

_____

_____

_____

_____

_____

_____

_____

_____

_____

_____

_____

_____

_____

EXERCISE 4-12

Balance Sheet

Chapter 4

EXERCISE 4-13

Name _____

EXERCISE 4-13, Concluded

Chapter 4

Balance Sheet

EXERCISE 4-14

a. Accounts Payable: _____

b. Accumulated Depreciation—Equipment: _____

c. Depreciation Expense—Equipment: _____

d. Equipment: _____

e. Fauzi Hanna, Capital: _____

f. Fauzi Hanna, Drawing: _____

g. Fees Earned: _____

h. Land: _____

i. Supplies: _____

j. Supplies Expense: _____

k. Wages Expense: _____

l. Wages Payable: _____

EXERCISE 4-15

_____

_____

_____

_____

_____

EXERCISE 4-16

a.

JOURNAL   PAGE

	DATE		DESCRIPTION	POST. REF.	DEBIT	CREDIT	
1							1
2							2
3							3
4							4
5							5
6							6
7							6
8							8

b. _____

EXERCISE 4-17

JOURNAL   PAGE

	DATE		DESCRIPTION	POST. REF.	DEBIT	CREDIT	
1							1
2							2
3							3
4							4
5							5
6							6
7							7
8							8
9							9
10							10
11							11
12							12
13							13
14							14

EXERCISE 4-18

a. Accounts Payable: _____

b. Accumulated Depreciation: _____

c. Anthony Adams, Capital: _____

d. Anthony Adams, Drawing: _____

e. Cash: _____

f. Depreciation Expense: _____

g. Fees Earned: _____

h. Office Equipment: _____

i. Salaries Expense: _____

j. Salaries Payable: _____

k. Supplies: _____

EXERCISE 4-19

Post-Closing Trial Balance		

EXERCISE 4-20

1. _____   6. _____
2. _____   7. _____
3. _____   8. _____
4. _____   9. _____
5. _____   10. _____

EXERCISE 4-21

a.

	December 31,	
	2008	**2007**
_____	_____	_____
_____	_____	_____
Working capital	_____	_____
Current ratio	_____	_____

b.

_____
_____
_____
_____
_____
_____

EXERCISE 4-22

a.

	Sept. 27, 2009	**Sept. 28, 2008**
_____	_____	_____
_____	_____	_____
Working capital	_____	_____
Current ratio	_____	_____

b.

_____
_____
_____
_____
_____
_____

APPENDIX EXERCISE 4-23

1. _____

2. _____

3. _____

4. _____

5. _____

6. _____

7. _____

8. _____

9. _____

10. _____

APPENDIX EXERCISE 4-24

Zeidman Security Services Co.
End-of-Period Spreadsheet (Work Sheet)
For the Year Ended July 31, 2012

	A	Unadjusted Trial Balance		Adjustments		Adjusted Trial Balance		Income Statement		Balance Sheet	
	Account Title	Dr.	Cr.	Dr.	Cr.	Dr.	Cr.	Dr.	Cr.	Dr.	Cr.
1											
2											
3											
4											
5											
6	Account Title										
7	Cash	12									
8	Accounts Receivable	80									
9	Supplies	8									
10	Prepaid Insurance	12									
11	Land	100									
12	Equipment	40									
13	Accumulated Depr. — Equip.		4								
14	Accounts Payable		36								
15	Wages Payable		0								
16	Alex Zeidman, Capital		170								
17	Alex Zeidman, Drawing	8									
18	Fees Earned		90								
19	Wages Expense	20									
20	Rent Expense	12									
21	Insurance Expense	0									
22	Utilities Expense	6									
23	Depreciation Expense	0									
24	Supplies Expense	0									
25	Miscellaneous Expense	2									
26	Totals	300	300								
27											
28											
29											
30											
31											
32											

Name _____

APPENDIX EXERCISE 4-25

Zeidman Security Services Co.
End-of-Period Spreadsheet (Work Sheet)
For the Year Ended July 31, 2012

	Unadjusted Trial Balance		Adjustments		Adjusted Trial Balance		Income Statement		Balance Sheet	
Account Title	Dr.	Cr.	Dr.	Cr.	Dr.	Cr.	Dr.	Cr.	Dr.	Cr.
Cash					12					
Accounts Receivable					89					
Supplies					3					
Prepaid Insurance					4					
Land					100					
Equipment					40					
Accumulated Depr. — Equip.						8				
Accounts Payable						36				
Wages Payable						1				
Alex Zeidman, Capital						170				
Alex Zeidman, Drawing					8					
Fees Earned						99				
Wages Expense					21					
Rent Expense					12					
Insurance Expense					8					
Utilities Expense					6					
Supplies Expense					5					
Depreciation Expense					4					
Miscellaneous Expense					2					
Totals					314	314				
Net income (loss)										

APPENDIX EXERCISE 4-26

Income Statement

Statement of Owner's Equity

APPENDIX EXERCISE 4-26, Concluded

Balance Sheet

APPENDIX EXERCISE 4-27

JOURNAL

	DATE		DESCRIPTION	POST. REF.	DEBIT	CREDIT	
1							1
2							2
3							3
4							4
5							5
6							6
7							7
8							8
9							9
10							10
11							11
12							12
13							13
14							14
15							15
16							16
17							17
18							18
19							19
20							20

APPENDIX EXERCISE 4-28

JOURNAL   PAGE

	DATE		DESCRIPTION	POST. REF.	DEBIT	CREDIT	
1							1
2							2
3							3
4							4
5							5
6							6
7							7
8							8
9							9
10							10
11							11
12							12
13							13
14							14
15							15
16							16
17							17
18							18
19							19
20							20

PROBLEM 4-1 ___

1.

	Income Statement				

2.

Statement of Owner's Equity		

Name _____

PROBLEM 4-1 ____, Continued

3.

Balance Sheet

PROBLEM 4-1 ___ , Continued

4.

		JOURNAL				PAGE

	DATE	DESCRIPTION	POST. REF.	DEBIT	CREDIT	
1						1
2						2
3						3
4						4
5						5
6						6
7						7
8						8
9						9
10						10
11						11
12						12
13						13
14						14
15						15
16						16
17						17
18						18
19						19
20						20
21						21
22						22
23						23
24						24
25						25
26						26
27						27
28						28
29						29
30						30
31						31
32						32
33						33
34						34
35						35
36						36

PROBLEM 4-1 ___, Concluded

5.

Post-Closing Trial Balance		

PROBLEM 4-2 ___

1.

	Income Statement		

	Statement of Owner's Equity		

Name _____

PROBLEM 4-2 ____, **Continued**

Balance Sheet

PROBLEM 4-2 ___, Concluded

2.

JOURNAL   PAGE

	DATE		DESCRIPTION	POST. REF.	DEBIT	CREDIT	
1							1
2							2
3							3
4							4
5							5
6							6
7							7
8							8
9							9
10							10
11							11
12							12
13							13
14							14
15							15
16							16
17							17
18							18
19							19
20							20
21							21

3.

_____

_____

_____

_____

_____

_____

_____

_____

_____

_____

_____

This Page Not Used.

PROBLEM 4-3 ___

1., 3., and 6.

Cash

Laundry Supplies

Prepaid Insurance

Laundry Equipment

Accumulated Depreciation

Accounts Payable

Wages Payable

_____, *Capital*

PROBLEM 4-3 ___, Continued

_____ *, Drawing*

Income Summary

Laundry Revenue

Wages Expense

Rent Expense

Utilities Expense

Depreciation Expense

Laundry Supplies Expense

Insurance Expense

Miscellaneous Expense

PROBLEM 4-3 ____, Continued

2. Optional (Appendix)

End-of-Period Spreadsheet (Work Sheet)

	A		B	C		D	E		F	G		H	I		J	K
	Account Title		Unadjusted Trial Balance			Adjustments			Adjusted Trial Balance			Income Statement			Balance Sheet	
			Dr.	Cr.		Dr.	Cr.		Dr.	Cr.		Dr.	Cr.		Dr.	Cr.
1																
2																
3																
4																
5																
6																
7																
8																
9																
10																
11																
12																
13																
14																
15																
16																
17																
18																
19																
20																
21																
22																
23																
24																
25																
26																
27																
28																
29																
30																

PROBLEM 4-3 ___, Continued

3.

JOURNAL

	DATE		DESCRIPTION	POST. REF.	DEBIT	CREDIT	
1			*Adjusting Entries*				1
2							2
3							3
4							4
5							5
6							6
7							7
8							8
9							9
10							10
11							11
12							12
13							13
14							14
15							15
16							16
17							17
18							18
19							19
20							20
21							21
22							22
23							23
24							24
25							25
26							26
27							27
28							28
29							29
30							30
31							31
32							32
33							33
34							34
35							35
36							36

PROBLEM 4-3 ___, Continued

4.

	Adjusted Trial Balance		

PROBLEM 4-3 ___, Continued

5.

Income Statement

Statement of Owner's Equity

Name _____

PROBLEM 4-3 _____, Continued

Balance Sheet

PROBLEM 4-3 ___ , Concluded

6.

JOURNAL

	DATE		DESCRIPTION	POST. REF.	DEBIT	CREDIT	
1			*Closing Entries*				1
2							2
3							3
4							4
5							5
6							6
7							7
8							8
9							9
10							10
11							11
12							12
13							13
14							14
15							15
16							16
17							17
18							18
19							19

7.

Post-Closing Trial Balance

PROBLEM 4-4 _____

1. Optional (Appendix)

End-of-Period Spreadsheet (Work Sheet)

	A	Unadjusted Trial Balance Dr.	Cr.	Adjustments Dr.	Cr.	Adjusted Trial Balance Dr.	Cr.	Income Statement Dr.	Cr.	Balance Sheet Dr.	Cr.
1											
2											
3											
4											
5											
6	Account Title										
7	Cash	26,750									
8	Accounts Receivable	10,900									
9	Supplies	5,400									
10	Prepaid Insurance	4,800									
11	Land	50,000									
12	Building	57,500									
13	Accum. Depr.—Building		23,400								
14	Equipment	32,000									
15	Accum. Depr.—Equipment		10,200								
16	Accounts Payable		3,350								
17	Wages Payable										
18	Unearned Rent		2,700								
19	Lee Watts, Capital		125,350								
20	Lee Watts, Drawing	2,000									
21	Service Revenue		35,000								
22	Rent Revenue										
23	Wages Expense	5,000									
24	Rent Expense	2,500									
25	Utilities Expense	1,650									
26	Supplies Expense										
27	Depr. Exp.—Building										
28	Insurance Expense										
29	Depr. Exp.—Equipment										
30	Misc. Expense	1,500									
31		200,000	200,000								
32											
33											
34											

PROBLEM 4-4 ___, Continued

2.

	JOURNAL			PAGE 26

	DATE		DESCRIPTION	POST. REF.	DEBIT	CREDIT	
1			*Adjusting Entries*				1
2							2
3							3
4							4
5							5
6							6
7							7
8							8
9							9
10							10
11							11
12							12
13							13
14							14
15							15
16							16
17							17
18							18
19							19
20							20
21							21
22							22
23							23
24							24
25							25
26							26
27							27
28							28
29							29
30							30
31							31
32							32
33							33
34							34
35							35
36							36

PROBLEM 4-4 ___, Continued

3.

	Adjusted Trial Balance		

PROBLEM 4-4 ___, Continued

4.

	Income Statement		

	Statement of Owner's Equity		

PROBLEM 4-4 _____, Continued

Balance Sheet

PROBLEM 4-4 ___ , Continued

5.

JOURNAL

PAGE 27

	DATE		DESCRIPTION	POST. REF.	DEBIT	CREDIT	
1			*Closing Entries*				1
2							2
3							3
4							4
5							5
6							6
7							7
8							8
9							9
10							10
11							11
12							12
13							13
14							14
15							15
16							16
17							17
18							18
19							19
20							20
21							21
22							22
23							23
24							24
25							25
26							26
27							27
28							28
29							29
30							30
31							31
32							32
33							33
34							34
35							35
36							36

PROBLEM 4-4 ___, Continued

6.

Post-Closing Trial Balance		

PROBLEM 4-4 ___, Continued

2. and 5.

ACCOUNT   *Cash*   ACCOUNT NO.   *11*

DATE		ITEM	POST. REF.	DEBIT	CREDIT	BALANCE DEBIT	BALANCE CREDIT
2012 July	1	Balance	√			6,000.00	
	3		23		2,500.00	3,500.00	
	4		23	5,000.00		8,500.00	
	5		23		400.00	8,100.00	
	7		23	3,200.00		11,300.00	
	8		23	5,900.00		17,200.00	
	8		23		4,500.00	12,700.00	
	8		23	9,400.00		22,100.00	
	10		24		500.00	21,600.00	
	12		24		2,400.00	19,200.00	
	15		24	7,800.00		27,000.00	
	16		24		1,000.00	26,000.00	
	19		24		2,100.00	23,900.00	
	22		24		1,200.00	22,700.00	
	22		24	8,100.00		30,800.00	
	24		25		800.00	30,000.00	
	26		25		2,600.00	27,400.00	
	30		25		350.00	27,050.00	
	30		25		600.00	26,450.00	
	31		25		1,000.00	25,450.00	
	31		25	2,200.00		27,650.00	
	31		25		900.00	26,750.00	

PROBLEM 4-4 ___ , Continued

ACCOUNT   *Accounts Receivable*   ACCOUNT NO.   12

DATE		ITEM	POST. REF.	DEBIT	CREDIT	BALANCE DEBIT	BALANCE CREDIT
2012 July	1	Balance	√			12,500.00	
	7		23		3,200.00	9,300.00	
	8		23		5,900.00	3,400.00	
	22		24	7,500.00		10,900.00	

ACCOUNT   *Supplies*   ACCOUNT NO.   13

DATE		ITEM	POST. REF.	DEBIT	CREDIT	BALANCE DEBIT	BALANCE CREDIT
2012 July	1	Balance	√			4,100.00	
	10		24	500.00		4,600.00	
	27		25	800.00		5,400.00	

ACCOUNT   *Prepaid Insurance*   ACCOUNT NO.   14

DATE		ITEM	POST. REF.	DEBIT	CREDIT	BALANCE DEBIT	BALANCE CREDIT
2012 July y	1	Balance	√			3,600.00	
	22		24	1,200.00		4,800.00	

ACCOUNT   *Land*   ACCOUNT NO.   15

DATE		ITEM	POST. REF.	DEBIT	CREDIT	BALANCE DEBIT	BALANCE CREDIT
2012 July	1	Balance	√			50,000.00	

PROBLEM 4-4 ___ , Continued

ACCOUNT   *Building*   ACCOUNT NO.   16

DATE		ITEM	POST. REF.	DEBIT	CREDIT	BALANCE DEBIT	BALANCE CREDIT
2012 July	1	Balance	√			57,500.00	

ACCOUNT   *Accumulated Depreciation—Building*   ACCOUNT NO.   17

DATE		ITEM	POST. REF.	DEBIT	CREDIT	BALANCE DEBIT	BALANCE CREDIT
2012 July	1	Balance	√				23,400.00

ACCOUNT   *Equipment*   ACCOUNT NO.   18

DATE		ITEM	POST. REF.	DEBIT	CREDIT	BALANCE DEBIT	BALANCE CREDIT
2012 July	1	Balance	√			29,250.00	
	3		23	2,750.00		32,000.00	

ACCOUNT   *Accumulated Depreciation—Equipment*   ACCOUNT NO.   19

DATE		ITEM	POST. REF.	DEBIT	CREDIT	BALANCE DEBIT	BALANCE CREDIT
2012 July	1	Balance	√				10,200.00

PROBLEM 4-4 ___, Continued

ACCOUNT   *Accounts Payable*   ACCOUNT NO.   *21*

DATE		ITEM	POST. REF.	DEBIT	CREDIT	BALANCE DEBIT	BALANCE CREDIT
2012 July	1	Balance	√				6,300.00
	3		23		2,750.00		9,050.00
	8		23	4,500.00			4,550.00
	19		24	2,100.00			2,450.00
	31		25		900.00		3,350.00

ACCOUNT   *Wages Payable*   ACCOUNT NO.   *22*

DATE		ITEM	POST. REF.	DEBIT	CREDIT	BALANCE DEBIT	BALANCE CREDIT

ACCOUNT   *Unearned Rent*   ACCOUNT NO.   *23*

DATE		ITEM	POST. REF.	DEBIT	CREDIT	BALANCE DEBIT	BALANCE CREDIT
2012 July	1	Balance	√				2,700.00

ACCOUNT   *Lee Watts, Capital*   ACCOUNT NO.   *31*

DATE		ITEM	POST. REF.	DEBIT	CREDIT	BALANCE DEBIT	BALANCE CREDIT
2010 July	1	Balance	√				120,350.00
	4	23	23		5,000.00		125,350.00

PROBLEM 4-4 ___ , Continued

ACCOUNT   *Lee Watts, Drawing*   ACCOUNT NO.   *32*

DATE		ITEM	POST. REF.	DEBIT	CREDIT	BALANCE	
						DEBIT	CREDIT
2012 July	16		24	1,000.00		1,000.00	
	31		25	1,000.00		2,000.00	

ACCOUNT   *Income Summary*   ACCOUNT NO.   *33*

DATE	ITEM	POST. REF.	DEBIT	CREDIT	BALANCE	
					DEBIT	CREDIT

ACCOUNT   *Service Revenue*   ACCOUNT NO.   *41*

DATE		ITEM	POST. REF.	DEBIT	CREDIT	BALANCE	
						DEBIT	CREDIT
2012 July	8		23		9,400.00		9,400.00
	15		24		7,800.00		17,200.00
	22		24		8,100.00		25,300.00
	22		24		7,500.00		32,800.00
	31		25		2,200.00		35,000.00

PROBLEM 4-4 ___, Continued

ACCOUNT   *Rent Revenue*   ACCOUNT NO.   42

DATE	ITEM	POST. REF.	DEBIT	CREDIT	BALANCE DEBIT	BALANCE CREDIT

ACCOUNT   *Wages Expense*   ACCOUNT NO.   51

DATE		ITEM	POST. REF.	DEBIT	CREDIT	BALANCE DEBIT	BALANCE CREDIT
2012 July	12		24	2,400.00		2,400.00	
	26		25	2,600.00		5,000.00	

ACCOUNT   *Rent Expense*   ACCOUNT NO.   52

DATE		ITEM	POST. REF.	DEBIT	CREDIT	BALANCE DEBIT	BALANCE CREDIT
2012 July	3		23	2,500.00		2,500.00	

ACCOUNT   *Utilities Expense*   ACCOUNT NO.   53

DATE		ITEM	POST. REF.	DEBIT	CREDIT	BALANCE DEBIT	BALANCE CREDIT
2012 July	5		24	400.00		400.00	
	30		25	350.00		750.00	
	31		25	900.00		1,650.00	

PROBLEM 4-4 ___,   Continued

ACCOUNT   *Supplies Expense*   ACCOUNT NO.   54

DATE		ITEM	POST. REF.	DEBIT	CREDIT	BALANCE	
						DEBIT	CREDIT

ACCOUNT   *Depreciation Expense—Building*   ACCOUNT NO.   55

DATE		ITEM	POST. REF.	DEBIT	CREDIT	BALANCE	
						DEBIT	CREDIT

ACCOUNT   *Insurance Expense*   ACCOUNT NO.   56

DATE		ITEM	POST. REF.	DEBIT	CREDIT	BALANCE	
						DEBIT	CREDIT

ACCOUNT   *Depreciation Expense—Equipment*   ACCOUNT NO.   57

DATE		ITEM	POST. REF.	DEBIT	CREDIT	BALANCE	
						DEBIT	CREDIT

PROBLEM 4-4 ___, Concluded

ACCOUNT   *Miscellaneous Expense*   ACCOUNT NO.   *59*

DATE		ITEM	POST. REF.	DEBIT	CREDIT	BALANCE	
						DEBIT	CREDIT
2012 July	30		25	600.00		600.00	
	31		25	900.00		1,500.00	

This Page Not Used.

PROBLEM 4-5 _____

2. Optional (Appendix)

	A	B	C	D	E	F	G	H	I	J	K
		End-of-Period Spreadsheet (Work Sheet)									
		Unadjusted Trial Balance		Adjustments		Adjusted Trial Balance		Income Statement		Balance Sheet	
6	Account Title	Dr.	Cr.	Dr.	Cr.	Dr.	Cr.	Dr.	Cr.	Dr.	Cr.
1											
2											
3											
4											
5											
7											
8											
9											
10											
11											
12											
13											
14											
15											
16											
17											
18											
19											
20											
21											
22											
23											
24											
25											
26											
27											
28											
29											
30											
31											
32											

PROBLEM 4-5 ___ , Continued

3.

JOURNAL   PAGE *26*

	DATE		DESCRIPTION	POST. REF.	DEBIT	CREDIT	
1			*Adjusting Entries*				1
2							2
3							3
4							4
5							5
6							6
7							7
8							8
9							9
10							10
11							11
12							12
13							13
14							14
15							15
16							16
17							17
18							18
19							19
20							20
21							21
22							22
23							23
24							24
25							25
26							26
27							27
28							28
29							29
30							30
31							31
32							32
33							33
34							34
35							35
36							36

PROBLEM 4-5 ___, Continued

4.

	Adjusted Trial Balance		

PROBLEM 4-5 ___ , Continued

5.

Income Statement		

Statement of Owner's Equity		

Name _____

PROBLEM 4-5 ____, Continued

Chapter 4

Balance Sheet

PROBLEM 4-5 ___ , Continued

1., 3., and 6.

ACCOUNT   *Cash*   ACCOUNT NO.   11

DATE		ITEM	POST. REF.	DEBIT	CREDIT	BALANCE	
						DEBIT	CREDIT

ACCOUNT   *Supplies*   ACCOUNT NO.   13

DATE		ITEM	POST. REF.	DEBIT	CREDIT	BALANCE	
						DEBIT	CREDIT

ACCOUNT   *Prepaid Insurance*   ACCOUNT NO.   14

DATE		ITEM	POST. REF.	DEBIT	CREDIT	BALANCE	
						DEBIT	CREDIT

ACCOUNT   *Equipment*   ACCOUNT NO.   16

DATE		ITEM	POST. REF.	DEBIT	CREDIT	BALANCE	
						DEBIT	CREDIT

ACCOUNT   *Accumulated Depreciation—Equipment*   ACCOUNT NO.   17

DATE		ITEM	POST. REF.	DEBIT	CREDIT	BALANCE	
						DEBIT	CREDIT

PROBLEM 4-5 ___, Continued

ACCOUNT *Trucks*   ACCOUNT NO. 18

DATE	ITEM	POST. REF.	DEBIT	CREDIT	BALANCE DEBIT	BALANCE CREDIT

ACCOUNT *Accumulated Depreciation—Trucks*   ACCOUNT NO. 19

DATE	ITEM	POST. REF.	DEBIT	CREDIT	BALANCE DEBIT	BALANCE CREDIT

ACCOUNT *Accounts Payable*   ACCOUNT NO. 21

DATE	ITEM	POST. REF.	DEBIT	CREDIT	BALANCE DEBIT	BALANCE CREDIT

ACCOUNT *Wages Payable*   ACCOUNT NO. 22

DATE	ITEM	POST. REF.	DEBIT	CREDIT	BALANCE DEBIT	BALANCE CREDIT

ACCOUNT _____, *Capital*   ACCOUNT NO. 31

DATE	ITEM	POST. REF.	DEBIT	CREDIT	BALANCE DEBIT	BALANCE CREDIT

ACCOUNT _____, *Drawing*   ACCOUNT NO. 32

DATE	ITEM	POST. REF.	DEBIT	CREDIT	BALANCE DEBIT	BALANCE CREDIT

PROBLEM 4-5 ___, Continued

ACCOUNT   *Income Summary*   ACCOUNT NO.   33

DATE	ITEM	POST. REF.	DEBIT	CREDIT	BALANCE DEBIT	BALANCE CREDIT

ACCOUNT   *Service Revenue*   ACCOUNT NO.   41

DATE	ITEM	POST. REF.	DEBIT	CREDIT	BALANCE DEBIT	BALANCE CREDIT

ACCOUNT   *Wages Expense*   ACCOUNT NO.   51

DATE	ITEM	POST. REF.	DEBIT	CREDIT	BALANCE DEBIT	BALANCE CREDIT

ACCOUNT   *Supplies Expense*   ACCOUNT NO.

DATE	ITEM	POST. REF.	DEBIT	CREDIT	BALANCE DEBIT	BALANCE CREDIT

ACCOUNT   *Rent Expense*   ACCOUNT NO.

DATE	ITEM	POST. REF.	DEBIT	CREDIT	BALANCE DEBIT	BALANCE CREDIT

PROBLEM 4-5 ___ , Continued

ACCOUNT *Depreciation Expense—Equipment* ACCOUNT NO. _____

DATE	ITEM	POST. REF.	DEBIT	CREDIT	BALANCE	
					DEBIT	CREDIT

ACCOUNT *Truck Expense* ACCOUNT NO. _____

DATE	ITEM	POST. REF.	DEBIT	CREDIT	BALANCE	
					DEBIT	CREDIT

ACCOUNT *Depreciation Expense—Trucks* ACCOUNT NO. *56*

DATE	ITEM	POST. REF.	DEBIT	CREDIT	BALANCE	
					DEBIT	CREDIT

ACCOUNT *Insurance Expense* ACCOUNT NO. *57*

DATE	ITEM	POST. REF.	DEBIT	CREDIT	BALANCE	
					DEBIT	CREDIT

ACCOUNT *Miscellaneous Expense* ACCOUNT NO. *59*

DATE	ITEM	POST. REF.	DEBIT	CREDIT	BALANCE	
					DEBIT	CREDIT

PROBLEM 4-5 ___ , Concluded

6.

JOURNAL   PAGE *27*

	DATE		DESCRIPTION	POST. REF.	DEBIT	CREDIT	
1			*Closing Entries*				1
2							2
3							3
4							4
5							5
6							6
7							7
8							8
9							9
10							10
11							11
12							12
13							13
14							14
15							15
16							16
17							17
18							18
19							19
20							20

7.

Post-Closing Trial Balance

PROBLEM 4-6 ___

1. and 2. **JOURNAL** PAGE *1*

	DATE		DESCRIPTION	POST. REF.	DEBIT	CREDIT	
1							1
2							2
3							3
4							4
5							5
6							6
7							7
8							8
9							9
10							10
11							11
12							12
13							13
14							14
15							15
16							16
17							17
18							18
19							19
20							20
21							21
22							22
23							23
24							24
25							25
26							26
27							27
28							28
29							29
30							30
31							31
32							32
33							33
34							34
35							35
36							36

PROBLEM 4-6 ___, Continued

		JOURNAL			PAGE 2

	DATE	DESCRIPTION	POST. REF.	DEBIT	CREDIT	
1						1
2						2
3						3
4						4
5						5
6						6
7						7
8						8
9						9
10						10
11						11
12						12
13						13
14						14
15						15
16						16
17						17
18						18
19						19
20						20
21						21
22						22
23						23
24						24
25						25
26						26
27						27
28						28
29						29
30						30
31						31
32						32
33						33
34						34
35						35
36						36

PROBLEM 4-6 ___ , Continued

2., 6., and 9.

ACCOUNT   *Cash*   ACCOUNT NO.   *11*

DATE		ITEM	POST. REF.	DEBIT	CREDIT	BALANCE	
						DEBIT	CREDIT

ACCOUNT   *Accounts Receivable*   ACCOUNT NO.   *12*

DATE		ITEM	POST. REF.	DEBIT	CREDIT	BALANCE	
						DEBIT	CREDIT

PROBLEM 4-6 ___ , Continued

ACCOUNT   *Supplies*   ACCOUNT NO.   14

DATE		ITEM	POST. REF.	DEBIT	CREDIT	BALANCE	
						DEBIT	CREDIT

ACCOUNT   *Prepaid Rent*   ACCOUNT NO.   15

DATE		ITEM	POST. REF.	DEBIT	CREDIT	BALANCE	
						DEBIT	CREDIT

ACCOUNT   *Prepaid Insurance*   ACCOUNT NO.   16

DATE		ITEM	POST. REF.	DEBIT	CREDIT	BALANCE	
						DEBIT	CREDIT

ACCOUNT   *Office Equipment*   ACCOUNT NO.   18

DATE		ITEM	POST. REF.	DEBIT	CREDIT	BALANCE	
						DEBIT	CREDIT

ACCOUNT   *Accumulated Depreciation*   ACCOUNT NO.   19

DATE		ITEM	POST. REF.	DEBIT	CREDIT	BALANCE	
						DEBIT	CREDIT

PROBLEM 4-6 ___ , Continued

ACCOUNT   *Accounts Payable*   ACCOUNT NO.   21

DATE	ITEM	POST. REF.	DEBIT	CREDIT	BALANCE DEBIT	BALANCE CREDIT

ACCOUNT   *Salaries Payable*   ACCOUNT NO.   22

DATE	ITEM	POST. REF.	DEBIT	CREDIT	BALANCE DEBIT	BALANCE CREDIT

ACCOUNT   *Unearned Fees*   ACCOUNT NO.   23

DATE	ITEM	POST. REF.	DEBIT	CREDIT	BALANCE DEBIT	BALANCE CREDIT

ACCOUNT   _____, *Capital*   ACCOUNT NO.   31

DATE	ITEM	POST. REF.	DEBIT	CREDIT	BALANCE DEBIT	BALANCE CREDIT

ACCOUNT   _____, *Drawing*   ACCOUNT NO.   32

DATE	ITEM	POST. REF.	DEBIT	CREDIT	BALANCE DEBIT	BALANCE CREDIT

PROBLEM 4-6 ___ , Continued

ACCOUNT   *Income Summary*   ACCOUNT NO.   33

DATE		ITEM	POST. REF.	DEBIT	CREDIT	BALANCE	
						DEBIT	CREDIT

ACCOUNT   *Fees Earned*   ACCOUNT NO.   41

DATE		ITEM	POST. REF.	DEBIT	CREDIT	BALANCE	
						DEBIT	CREDIT

ACCOUNT   *Salary Expense*   ACCOUNT NO.   51

DATE		ITEM	POST. REF.	DEBIT	CREDIT	BALANCE	
						DEBIT	CREDIT

ACCOUNT   *Rent Expense*   ACCOUNT NO.

DATE		ITEM	POST. REF.	DEBIT	CREDIT	BALANCE	
						DEBIT	CREDIT

PROBLEM 4-6 ___, Continued

ACCOUNT   *Supplies Expense*   ACCOUNT NO. _____

| DATE | | ITEM | POST. REF. | DEBIT | CREDIT | BALANCE | |
						DEBIT	CREDIT

ACCOUNT   *Depreciation Expense*   ACCOUNT NO. *54*

| DATE | | ITEM | POST. REF. | DEBIT | CREDIT | BALANCE | |
						DEBIT	CREDIT

ACCOUNT   *Insurance Expense*   ACCOUNT NO. *55*

| DATE | | ITEM | POST. REF. | DEBIT | CREDIT | BALANCE | |
						DEBIT	CREDIT

ACCOUNT   *Miscellaneous Expense*   ACCOUNT NO. *59*

| DATE | | ITEM | POST. REF. | DEBIT | CREDIT | BALANCE | |
						DEBIT	CREDIT

PROBLEM 4-6 ___ , Continued

3.

Unadjusted Trial Balance		

PROBLEM 4-6 ___, Continued

6. JOURNAL PAGE 3

	DATE		DESCRIPTION	POST. REF.	DEBIT	CREDIT	
1			*Adjusting Entries*				1
2							2
3							3
4							4
5							5
6							6
7							7
8							8
9							9
10							10
11							11
12							12
13							13
14							14
15							15
16							16
17							17
18							18
19							19
20							20
21							21
22							22
23							23
24							24
25							25
26							26
27							27
28							28
29							29
30							30
31							31
32							32
33							33
34							34
35							35
36							36

PROBLEM 4-6 ___, Continued

7.

Adjusted Trial Balance

PROBLEM 4-6 ___, Continued

8.

Income Statement

Statement of Owner's Equity

Name _____

PROBLEM 4-6 ____, Continued

Balance Sheet

PROBLEM 4-6 _____, Continued

5. Optional (Appendix)

End-of-Period Spreadsheet (Work Sheet)

	A	B	C	D	E	F	G	H	I	J	K
	Account Title	Unadjusted Trial Balance		Adjustments		Adjusted Trial Balance		Income Statement		Balance Sheet	
		Dr.	Cr.	Dr.	Cr.	Dr.	Cr.	Dr.	Cr.	Dr.	Cr.
1											
2											
3											
4											
5											
6											
7											
8											
9											
10											
11											
12											
13											
14											
15											
16											
17											
18											
19											
20											
21											
22											
23											
24											
25											
26											
27											
28											
29											
30											
31											
32											

PROBLEM 4-6 ___ , Concluded

9.   **JOURNAL**   PAGE   4

	DATE		DESCRIPTION	POST. REF.	DEBIT	CREDIT	
1			*Closing Entries*				1
2							2
3							3
4							4
5							5
6							6
7							7
8							8
9							9
10							10
11							11
12							12
13							13
14							14
15							15
16							16
17							17
18							18

10.

Post-Closing Trial Balance

CONTINUING PROBLEM

1. Optional (Appendix)

End-of-Period Spreadsheet (Work Sheet)

	A	B	C	D	E	F	G	H	I	J	K
	Account Title	Unadjusted Trial Balance		Adjustments		Adjusted Trial Balance		Income Statement		Balance Sheet	
		Dr.	Cr.	Dr.	Cr.	Dr.	Cr.	Dr.	Cr.	Dr.	Cr.
1											
2											
3											
4											
5											
6											
7											
8											
9											
10											
11											
12											
13											
14											
15											
16											
17											
18											
19											
20											
21											
22											
23											
24											
25											
26											
27											
28											
29											
30											
31											
32											

CONTINUING PROBLEM, Continued

2.

Income Statement

Statement of Owner's Equity

Name _____

CONTINUING PROBLEM, Continued

Chapter 4

Balance Sheet

CONTINUING PROBLEM, Continued

3. Note: Use the general ledger accounts provided in Chapter 3, page 116–121.

JOURNAL   PAGE 4

	DATE		DESCRIPTION	POST. REF.	DEBIT	CREDIT	
1			*Closing Entries*				1
2							2
3							3
4							4
5							5
6							6
7							7
8							8
9							9
10							10
11							11
12							12
13							13
14							14
15							15
16							16
17							17
18							18
19							19
20							20
21							21
22							22
23							23
24							24
25							25
26							26
27							27
28							28
29							29
30							30
31							31
32							32
33							33
34							34

CONTINUING PROBLEM, Concluded

4.

	Post-Closing Trial Balance		

This Page Not Used.

COMPREHENSIVE PROBLEM 1

1. and 2.

JOURNAL

	DATE		DESCRIPTION	POST. REF.	DEBIT	CREDIT	
1							1
2							2
3							3
4							4
5							5
6							6
7							7
8							8
9							9
10							10
11							11
12							12
13							13
14							14
15							15
16							16
17							17
18							18
19							19
20							20
21							21
22							22
23							23
24							24
25							25
26							26
27							27
28							28
29							29
30							30
31							31
32							32
33							33
34							34
35							35

COMPREHENSIVE PROBLEM 1, Continued

JOURNAL   PAGE *6*

	DATE		DESCRIPTION	POST. REF.	DEBIT	CREDIT	
1							1
2							2
3							3
4							4
5							5
6							6
7							7
8							8
9							9
10							10
11							11
12							12
13							13
14							14
15							15
16							16
17							17
18							18
19							19
20							20
21							21
22							22
23							23
24							24
25							25
26							26
27							27
28							28
29							29
30							30
31							31
32							32
33							33
34							34
35							35

COMPREHENSIVE PROBLEM 1, Continued

2., 6., and 9.

ACCOUNT   *Cash*   ACCOUNT NO.   11

DATE		ITEM	POST. REF.	DEBIT	CREDIT	BALANCE	
						DEBIT	CREDIT

ACCOUNT   *Accounts Receivable*   ACCOUNT NO.   12

DATE		ITEM	POST. REF.	DEBIT	CREDIT	BALANCE	
						DEBIT	CREDIT

ACCOUNT   *Supplies*   ACCOUNT NO.   14

DATE		ITEM	POST. REF.	DEBIT	CREDIT	BALANCE	
						DEBIT	CREDIT

COMPREHENSIVE PROBLEM 1, Continued

ACCOUNT *Prepaid Rent* ACCOUNT NO. 15

DATE		ITEM	POST. REF.	DEBIT	CREDIT	BALANCE	
						DEBIT	CREDIT

ACCOUNT *Prepaid Insurance* ACCOUNT NO. 16

DATE		ITEM	POST. REF.	DEBIT	CREDIT	BALANCE	
						DEBIT	CREDIT

ACCOUNT *Office Equipment* ACCOUNT NO. 18

DATE		ITEM	POST. REF.	DEBIT	CREDIT	BALANCE	
						DEBIT	CREDIT

ACCOUNT *Accumulated Depreciation* ACCOUNT NO. 19

DATE		ITEM	POST. REF.	DEBIT	CREDIT	BALANCE	
						DEBIT	CREDIT

ACCOUNT *Accounts Payable* ACCOUNT NO. 21

DATE		ITEM	POST. REF.	DEBIT	CREDIT	BALANCE	
						DEBIT	CREDIT

COMPREHENSIVE PROBLEM 1, Continued

ACCOUNT   *Salaries Payable*   ACCOUNT NO.   22

DATE		ITEM	POST. REF.	DEBIT	CREDIT	BALANCE	
						DEBIT	CREDIT

ACCOUNT   *Unearned Fees*   ACCOUNT NO.   23

DATE		ITEM	POST. REF.	DEBIT	CREDIT	BALANCE	
						DEBIT	CREDIT

ACCOUNT   *Kelly Pitney, Capital*   ACCOUNT NO.   31

DATE		ITEM	POST. REF.	DEBIT	CREDIT	BALANCE	
						DEBIT	CREDIT

ACCOUNT   *Kelly Pitney, Drawing*   ACCOUNT NO.   32

DATE		ITEM	POST. REF.	DEBIT	CREDIT	BALANCE	
						DEBIT	CREDIT

COMPREHENSIVE PROBLEM 1, Continued

ACCOUNT   *Income Summary*   ACCOUNT NO.   *33*

DATE	ITEM	POST. REF.	DEBIT	CREDIT	BALANCE DEBIT	CREDIT

ACCOUNT   *Fees Earned*   ACCOUNT NO.   *41*

DATE	ITEM	POST. REF.	DEBIT	CREDIT	BALANCE DEBIT	CREDIT

ACCOUNT   *Salary Expense*   ACCOUNT NO.   *51*

DATE	ITEM	POST. REF.	DEBIT	CREDIT	BALANCE DEBIT	CREDIT

ACCOUNT   *Rent Expense*   ACCOUNT NO.   *52*

DATE	ITEM	POST. REF.	DEBIT	CREDIT	BALANCE DEBIT	CREDIT

COMPREHENSIVE PROBLEM 1, Continued

ACCOUNT *Supplies Expense*   ACCOUNT NO. 53

DATE		ITEM	POST. REF.	DEBIT	CREDIT	BALANCE	
						DEBIT	CREDIT

ACCOUNT *Depreciation Expense*   ACCOUNT NO. 54

DATE		ITEM	POST. REF.	DEBIT	CREDIT	BALANCE	
						DEBIT	CREDIT

ACCOUNT *Insurance Expense*   ACCOUNT NO. 55

DATE		ITEM	POST. REF.	DEBIT	CREDIT	BALANCE	
						DEBIT	CREDIT

ACCOUNT *Miscellaneous Expense*   ACCOUNT NO. 59

DATE		ITEM	POST. REF.	DEBIT	CREDIT	BALANCE	
						DEBIT	CREDIT

COMPREHENSIVE PROBLEM 1, Continued

3.

	Unadjusted Trial Balance		

COMPREHENSIVE PROBLEM 1, Continued

5. Optional (Appendix)

End-of-Period Spreadsheet (Work Sheet)

	A	B	C	D	E	F	G	H	I	J	K
		Unadjusted Trial Balance		Adjustments		Adjusted Trial Balance		Income Statement		Balance Sheet	
	Account Title	Dr.	Cr.	Dr.	Cr.	Dr.	Cr.	Dr.	Cr.	Dr.	Cr.
1											
2											
3											
4											
5											
6											
7											
8											
9											
10											
11											
12											
13											
14											
15											
16											
17											
18											
19											
20											
21											
22											
23											
24											
25											
26											
27											
28											
29											
30											
31											
32											

COMPREHENSIVE PROBLEM 1, Continued

6.

JOURNAL

PAGE 7

	DATE		DESCRIPTION	POST. REF.	DEBIT	CREDIT	
1			*Adjusting Entries*				1
2							2
3							3
4							4
5							5
6							6
7							7
8							8
9							9
10							10
11							11
12							12
13							13
14							14
15							15
16							16
17							17
18							18
19							19
20							20
21							21
22							22
23							23
24							24
25							25
26							26
27							27
28							28
29							29
30							30
31							31
32							32
33							33
34							34

COMPREHENSIVE PROBLEM 1, Continued

7.

Adjusted Trial Balance		

COMPREHENSIVE PROBLEM 1, Continued

8.

Income Statement		

Statement of Owner's Equity		

COMPREHENSIVE PROBLEM 1, Continued

Balance Sheet

COMPREHENSIVE PROBLEM 1, Continued

9.

	DATE		DESCRIPTION	POST. REF.	DEBIT	CREDIT	
1			*Closing Entries*				1
2							2
3							3
4							4
5							5
6							6
7							7
8							8
9							9
10							10
11							11
12							12
13							13
14							14
15							15
16							16
17							17
18							18
19							19
20							20
21							21
22							22
23							23
24							24
25							25
26							26
27							27
28							28
29							29
30							30
31							31
32							32

JOURNAL   PAGE *8*

COMPREHENSIVE PROBLEM 1, Concluded

10.

Post-Closing Trial Balance		

This Page Not Used.

EXERCISE 5-1

REVENUE JOURNAL

Date	Invoice No.	Account Debited	Post. Ref.	Accounts Rec. Dr. Fees Earned Cr.
2012				
June 1	112	Haznat Safety Co.	(a) _____	$2,625
10	113	Masco Co.	(b) _____	980
18	114	Eco-Systems	(c) _____	1,600
27	115	Nero Enterprises	(d) _____	1,240
30				$6,445
			(e) _____	

EXERCISE 5-2

a., b., and c.

GENERAL LEDGER

ACCOUNTS RECEIVABLE SUBSIDIARY LEDGER

EXERCISE 5-2, Concluded

d.

Account Receivable Subsidiary Ledger		

EXERCISE 5-3

a. _____

b. _____

c. _____

d. _____

e. _____

f. _____

g. _____

h. _____

i. _____

j. _____

EXERCISE 5-4

a. _____

b. _____

c. _____

d. _____

e. _____

f. _____

g. _____

h. _____

i. _____

j. _____

k. _____

EXERCISE 5-5

Feb. 3 _____

   _____

   _____

Feb. 6 _____

   _____

   _____

Feb. 16 _____

   _____

   _____

EXERCISE 5-6

a.

REVENUE JOURNAL   PAGE

	DATE	INVOICE NO.	ACCOUNT DEBITED	POST. REF.	ACCTS. REC. DR. FEES EARNED CR.	
1						1
2						2
3						3
4						4
5						5
6						6
7						7
8						8
9						9
10						10
11						11
12						12
13						13
14						14
15						15

b.

_____

_____

c. _____

EXERCISE 5-7

a. and b.

Accounts Receivable—Astro Star Co.

Accounts Receivable—Bormann Co.

Accounts Receivable—Life Star Inc.

c.

Accounts Receivable

Fees Earned

d.

Accounts Receivable Subsidiary Ledger

EXERCISE 5-7, Concluded

e.

_____

_____

_____

_____

_____

_____

_____

_____

EXERCISE 5-8

Accounts Receivable Subsidiary Ledger

EXERCISE 5-8, Concluded

Accounts Receivable	
(Control)	

EXERCISE 5-9

REVENUE JOURNAL   PAGE 8

	DATE	INVOICE NO.	ACCOUNT DEBITED	POST. REF.	ACCTS. REC. DR. FEES EARNED CR.	
1						1
2						2
3						3
4						4
5						5
6						6
7						7
8						8
9						9
10						10
11						11
12						12
13						13
14						14
15						15

EXERCISE 5-9, Concluded

CASH RECEIPTS JOURNAL

	DATE		ACCOUNT CREDITED	POST. REF.	FEES EARNED CR.	ACCOUNTS REC. CR.	CASH DR.	
1								1
2								2
3								3
4								4
5								5
6								6
7								7
8								8
9								9
10								10
11								11
12								12
13								13
14								14
15								15

EXERCISE 5-10

a.

REVENUE JOURNAL   PAGE *19*

	DATE	INVOICE NO.	ACCOUNT DEBITED	POST. REF.	ACCTS. REC. DR. FEES EARNED CR.	
1						1
2						2
3						3
4						4
5						5
6						6
7						7
8						8
9						9
10						10
11						11
12						12
13						13
14						14
15						15

CASH RECEIPTS JOURNAL   PAGE *25*

	DATE	ACCOUNT CREDITED	POST. REF.	FEES EARNED CR.	ACCOUNTS REC. CR.	CASH DR.	
1							1
2							2
3							3
4							4
5							5
6							6
7							7
8							8
9							9
10							10
11							11
12							12
13							13
14							14
15							15

EXERCISE 5-10, Concluded

b.

Accounts Receivable Subsidiary Ledger

Accounts Receivable

c.

EXERCISE 5-11

a. _____

b. _____

c. _____

d. _____

e. _____

f. _____

g. _____

h. _____

i. _____

j. _____

k. _____

l. _____

m. _____

EXERCISE 5-12

a. _____

b. _____

c. _____

d. _____

e. _____

f. _____

g. _____

h. _____

i. _____

j. _____

k. _____

l. _____

EXERCISE 5-13

Mar. 6   _____

_____

Mar. 11   _____

_____

Mar. 16   _____

_____

235

EXERCISE 5-14

a.

PURCHASES JOURNAL

	DATE	ACCOUNT CREDITED	POST. REF.	ACCOUNTS PAYABLE CR.	OFFICE SUPPLIES DR.	OTHER ACCOUNTS DR.		
						ACCOUNT	POST. REF.	AMOUNT
1								1
2								2
3								3
4								4
5								5
6								6
7								7
8								8
9								9

b. _____

_____

c. _____

EXERCISE 5-15

a. and b.

Kleen-Mate Supplies Inc.

Little Co.

Office Mate Inc.

c.

Accounts Payable

Cleaning Supplies

d.

Accounts Payable Subsidiary Ledger

EXERCISE 5-15, Concluded

e.

_____

_____

_____

_____

_____

_____

_____

_____

EXERCISE 5-16

Accounts Payable Subsidiary Ledger

EXERCISE 5-16, Concluded

Accounts Payable	
(Control)	

EXERCISE 5-17

PURCHASES JOURNAL

PAGE 36

DATE	ACCOUNT CREDITED	POST. REF.	ACCOUNTS PAYABLE CR.	CLEANING SUPPLIES DR.	OTHER ACCOUNTS DR.		
					ACCOUNT	POST. REF.	AMOUNT
1							
2							
3							
4							
5							
6							
7							
8							
9							

CASH PAYMENTS JOURNAL

PAGE 41

DATE	CK. NO.	ACCOUNT DEBITED	POST. REF.	OTHER ACCOUNTS DR.	ACCOUNTS PAYABLE DR.	CASH CR.
1						
2						
3						
4						
5						
6						
7						
8						
9						

Name _____

EXERCISE 5-18

a.

PURCHASES JOURNAL

DATE	ACCOUNT CREDITED	POST. REF.	ACCOUNTS PAYABLE CR.	PET SUPPLIES DR.	OTHER ACCOUNTS DR.		
					ACCOUNT	POST. REF.	AMOUNT
1							
2							
3							
4							
5							
6							
7							
8							
9							

CASH PAYMENTS JOURNAL

DATE	CK. NO.	ACCOUNT DEBITED	POST. REF.	OTHER ACCOUNTS DR.	ACCOUNTS PAYABLE DR.	CASH CR.
1						
2						
3						
4						
5						
6						
7						
8						
9						

EXERCISE 5-18, Concluded

b.

Accounts Payable Subsidiary Ledger

Accounts Payable—Control

c.

EXERCISE 5-19

a.

_____
_____
_____
_____
_____
_____
_____
_____
_____
_____
_____
_____
_____
_____

b.

_____

Accounts Payable Subsidiary Ledger

EXERCISE 5-20

Revenue journal: _____

Cash receipts journal: _____

Purchases journal: _____

Cash payments journal: _____

General journal: _____

EXERCISE 5-21

_____

_____

_____

_____

_____

_____

_____

_____

_____

EXERCISE 5-22

a.

_____

_____

_____

_____

_____

_____

b.

_____

_____

_____

_____

_____

_____

EXERCISE 5-22, Concluded

c. _____

_____

_____

_____

_____

_____

_____

_____

_____

_____

_____

_____

_____

_____

_____

_____

EXERCISE 5-23

a.

_____

_____

_____

_____

b.   **JOURNAL**   PAGE *1*

	DATE		DESCRIPTION	POST. REF.	DEBIT	CREDIT	
1							1
2							2
3							3
4							4

c.

_____

_____

_____

_____

d.

_____

_____

_____

_____

e.

_____

_____

_____

_____

_____

_____

EXERCISE 5-24

a.

Amazon.com: _____

_____

b.

Dell Inc.: _____

_____

c.

DuPont.: _____

_____

d.

Intuit, Inc.: _____

_____

e.

L.L. Bean, Inc.: _____

_____

f.

W.W. Grainger, Inc.: _____

_____

EXERCISE 5-25

a.

	2009 (in millions)	2008 (in millions)	Increase (Decrease)	
			Amount	Percent

b.

	2009		2008	
	Amount	Percent	Amount	Percent

EXERCISE 5-25, Concluded

c. _____

_____

_____

_____

_____

_____

_____

_____

_____

_____

_____

_____

_____

EXERCISE 5-26

a.

Major Product Segments	Fiscal Year 2009 (in millions)	Percent	

b. _____

_____

_____

_____

_____

_____

_____

EXERCISE 5-27

a. Horizontal analysis:

	2009 (in millions)	2008 (in millions)	Increase (Decrease) Amount	Percent

b. Vertical analysis:

	2009 Amount (in millions)	Percent	2008 Amount (in millions)	Percent

c. _____

_____

_____

_____

_____

_____

_____

_____

_____

_____

PROBLEM 5-1 ___

1. and 2.

REVENUE JOURNAL   PAGE *1*

	DATE		INVOICE NO.	ACCOUNT DEBITED	POST. REF.	ACCTS. REC. DR. FEES EARNED CR.	
1							1
2							2
3							3
4							4
5							5
6							6
7							7
8							8
9							9
10							10
11							11

JOURNAL   PAGE *1*

	DATE		DESCRIPTION	POST. REF.	DEBIT	CREDIT	
1							1
2							2
3							3
4							4
5							5
6							6

PROBLEM 5-1 ___ , Continued

ACCOUNTS RECEIVABLE LEDGER

NAME

DATE		ITEM	POST. REF.	DEBIT	CREDIT	BALANCE

NAME

DATE		ITEM	POST. REF.	DEBIT	CREDIT	BALANCE

NAME

DATE		ITEM	POST. REF.	DEBIT	CREDIT	BALANCE

NAME

DATE		ITEM	POST. REF.	DEBIT	CREDIT	BALANCE

NAME

DATE		ITEM	POST. REF.	DEBIT	CREDIT	BALANCE

PROBLEM 5-1 ___ , Concluded

GENERAL LEDGER

2.

ACCOUNT _____   ACCOUNT NO. _____

DATE		ITEM	POST. REF.	DEBIT	CREDIT	BALANCE	
						DEBIT	CREDIT

ACCOUNT _____   ACCOUNT NO. _____

DATE		ITEM	POST. REF.	DEBIT	CREDIT	BALANCE	
						DEBIT	CREDIT

ACCOUNT _____   ACCOUNT NO. _____

DATE		ITEM	POST. REF.	DEBIT	CREDIT	BALANCE	
						DEBIT	CREDIT

3. a. _____

   b. _____

4.

_____

_____

_____

_____

_____

_____

_____

_____

252

This Page Not Used.

PROBLEM 5-2 ___

GENERAL LEDGER

1. and 5.

ACCOUNT _____   ACCOUNT NO. _____

DATE	ITEM	POST. REF.	DEBIT	CREDIT	BALANCE	
					DEBIT	CREDIT

ACCOUNT _____   ACCOUNT NO. _____

DATE	ITEM	POST. REF.	DEBIT	CREDIT	BALANCE	
					DEBIT	CREDIT

ACCOUNT _____   ACCOUNT NO. _____

DATE	ITEM	POST. REF.	DEBIT	CREDIT	BALANCE	
					DEBIT	CREDIT

ACCOUNT _____   ACCOUNT NO. _____

DATE	ITEM	POST. REF.	DEBIT	CREDIT	BALANCE	
					DEBIT	CREDIT

PROBLEM 5-2 ___, Continued

ACCOUNTS RECEIVABLE SUBSIDIARY LEDGER

2. and 4.

NAME

DATE		ITEM	POST. REF.	DEBIT	CREDIT	BALANCE

NAME

DATE		ITEM	POST. REF.	DEBIT	CREDIT	BALANCE

NAME

DATE		ITEM	POST. REF.	DEBIT	CREDIT	BALANCE

NAME

DATE		ITEM	POST. REF.	DEBIT	CREDIT	BALANCE

PROBLEM 5-2 __, Continued

3., 4., and 5.

REVENUE JOURNAL   PAGE *40*

	DATE	INVOICE NO.	ACCOUNT DEBITED	POST. REF.	ACCTS. REC. DR. FEES EARNED CR.	
1						1
2						2
3						3
4						4
5						5
14						14
15						15

CASH RECEIPTS JOURNAL   PAGE *36*

	DATE	ACCOUNT CREDITED	POST. REF.	FEES EARNED CR.	ACCOUNTS REC. CR.	CASH DR.	
1							1
2							2
3							3
4							4
5							5
6							6
19							19

JOURNAL   PAGE *1*

	DATE	DESCRIPTION	POST. REF.	DEBIT	CREDIT	
1						1
2						2
3						3
10						10

PROBLEM 5-2 ___ , Concluded

6. _____

_____

_____

7. _____

_____

_____

_____

_____

PROBLEM 5-3 ___

GENERAL LEDGER

1. and 4.

ACCOUNT *Field Supplies*   ACCOUNT NO. 14

DATE		ITEM	POST. REF.	DEBIT	CREDIT	BALANCE	
						DEBIT	CREDIT

ACCOUNT *Office Supplies*   ACCOUNT NO. 15

DATE		ITEM	POST. REF.	DEBIT	CREDIT	BALANCE	
						DEBIT	CREDIT

ACCOUNT *Office Equipment*   ACCOUNT NO. 18

DATE		ITEM	POST. REF.	DEBIT	CREDIT	BALANCE	
						DEBIT	CREDIT

ACCOUNT *Accounts Payable*   ACCOUNT NO. 21

DATE		ITEM	POST. REF.	DEBIT	CREDIT	BALANCE	
						DEBIT	CREDIT

PROBLEM 5-3 ___ , Continued

ACCOUNTS PAYABLE SUBSIDIARY LEDGER

2. and 3.

NAME _____

	DATE		ITEM	POST. REF.	DEBIT	CREDIT	BALANCE	

NAME _____

	DATE		ITEM	POST. REF.	DEBIT	CREDIT	BALANCE	

NAME _____

	DATE		ITEM	POST. REF.	DEBIT	CREDIT	BALANCE	

NAME _____

	DATE		ITEM	POST. REF.	DEBIT	CREDIT	BALANCE	

NAME _____

	DATE		ITEM	POST. REF.	DEBIT	CREDIT	BALANCE	

5. a. _____   **6.** _____

   b. _____   _____

PROBLEM 5-3 ____, Concluded

3. and 4.

PURCHASES JOURNAL

	DATE	ACCOUNT CREDITED	POST. REF.	ACCOUNTS PAYABLE CR.	FIELD SUPPLIES DR.	OFFICE SUPPLIES DR.	OTHER ACCOUNTS DR.			
							ACCOUNT	POST. REF.	AMOUNT	
1										1
2										2
3										3
4										4
5										5
6										6
7										7
8										8
9										9
10										10
11										11
12										12
13										13
14										14
15										15
16										16
17										17
18										18
19										19
20										20
21										21
22										22
23										23

This Page Not Used.

PROBLEM 5-4

1., 2., and 3.

PURCHASES JOURNAL

PAGE 1

	DATE	ACCOUNT CREDITED	POST. REF.	ACCOUNTS PAYABLE CR.	FIELD SUPPLIES DR.	OFFICE SUPPLIES DR.	OTHER ACCOUNTS DR.		
							ACCOUNT	POST. REF.	AMOUNT
1									
2									
3									
4									
5									
6									
7									
8									
9									
10									
11									
12									
13									
14									
15									
16									
17									
18									
19									
20									
21									
22									
23									

PROBLEM 5-4 ___, Continued

1., 2., and 3.

CASH PAYMENTS JOURNAL   PAGE 1

	DATE	CK. NO.	ACCOUNT DEBITED	POST. REF.	OTHER ACCOUNTS DR.	ACCOUNTS PAYABLE DR.	CASH CR.	
1								1
2								2
3								3
4								4
5								5
6								6
7								7
8								8
9								9
10								10
11								11
12								12
13								13
14								14
15								15
16								16
17								17

1. and 2.

JOURNAL   PAGE 1

	DATE	DESCRIPTION	POST. REF.	DEBIT	CREDIT	
1						1
2						2
3						3
4						4
5						5
6						6
7						7
8						8
9						9
10						10
11						11
12						12

PROBLEM 5-4 ___ , Continued

ACCOUNTS PAYABLE LEDGER

1.

NAME

DATE	ITEM	POST. REF.	DEBIT	CREDIT	BALANCE

NAME

DATE	ITEM	POST. REF.	DEBIT	CREDIT	BALANCE

NAME

DATE	ITEM	POST. REF.	DEBIT	CREDIT	BALANCE

PROBLEM 5-4 ___, Continued

GENERAL LEDGER

2. and 3.

ACCOUNT _____ ACCOUNT NO. _____

DATE		ITEM	POST. REF.	DEBIT	CREDIT	BALANCE	
						DEBIT	CREDIT

ACCOUNT _____ ACCOUNT NO. _____

DATE		ITEM	POST. REF.	DEBIT	CREDIT	BALANCE	
						DEBIT	CREDIT

ACCOUNT _____ ACCOUNT NO. _____

DATE		ITEM	POST. REF.	DEBIT	CREDIT	BALANCE	
						DEBIT	CREDIT

ACCOUNT _____ ACCOUNT NO. _____

DATE		ITEM	POST. REF.	DEBIT	CREDIT	BALANCE	
						DEBIT	CREDIT

ACCOUNT _____ ACCOUNT NO. _____

DATE		ITEM	POST. REF.	DEBIT	CREDIT	BALANCE	
						DEBIT	CREDIT

PROBLEM 5-4 ___ , Continued

ACCOUNT _____   ACCOUNT NO. _____

DATE	ITEM	POST. REF.	DEBIT	CREDIT	BALANCE	
					DEBIT	CREDIT

ACCOUNT _____   ACCOUNT NO. _____

DATE	ITEM	POST. REF.	DEBIT	CREDIT	BALANCE	
					DEBIT	CREDIT

ACCOUNT _____   ACCOUNT NO. _____

DATE	ITEM	POST. REF.	DEBIT	CREDIT	BALANCE	
					DEBIT	CREDIT

ACCOUNT _____   ACCOUNT NO. _____

DATE	ITEM	POST. REF.	DEBIT	CREDIT	BALANCE	
					DEBIT	CREDIT

ACCOUNT _____   ACCOUNT NO. _____

DATE	ITEM	POST. REF.	DEBIT	CREDIT	BALANCE	
					DEBIT	CREDIT

PROBLEM 5-4 ___, Concluded

4.

Accounts Payable Subsidiary Ledger		

5. _____

_____

_____

_____

PROBLEM 5-5 ___

GENERAL LEDGER

1., 3., and 4.

ACCOUNT   *Cash*   ACCOUNT NO.   *11*

DATE		ITEM	POST. REF.	DEBIT	CREDIT	BALANCE DEBIT	BALANCE CREDIT

ACCOUNT   *Accounts Receivable*   ACCOUNT NO.   *12*

DATE		ITEM	POST. REF.	DEBIT	CREDIT	BALANCE DEBIT	BALANCE CREDIT

ACCOUNT   *Maintenance Supplies*   ACCOUNT NO.   *14*

DATE		ITEM	POST. REF.	DEBIT	CREDIT	BALANCE DEBIT	BALANCE CREDIT

ACCOUNT   *Office Supplies*   ACCOUNT NO.   *15*

DATE		ITEM	POST. REF.	DEBIT	CREDIT	BALANCE DEBIT	BALANCE CREDIT

PROBLEM 5-5 ___ , Continued

ACCOUNT   *Office Equipment*   ACCOUNT NO.   16

DATE		ITEM	POST. REF.	DEBIT	CREDIT	BALANCE DEBIT	BALANCE CREDIT

ACCOUNT   *Accumulated Depreciation—Office Equipment*   ACCOUNT NO.   17

DATE		ITEM	POST. REF.	DEBIT	CREDIT	BALANCE DEBIT	BALANCE CREDIT

ACCOUNT   *Vehicles*   ACCOUNT NO.   18

DATE		ITEM	POST. REF.	DEBIT	CREDIT	BALANCE DEBIT	BALANCE CREDIT

ACCOUNT   *Accumulated Depreciation—Vehicles*   ACCOUNT NO.   19

DATE		ITEM	POST. REF.	DEBIT	CREDIT	BALANCE DEBIT	BALANCE CREDIT

PROBLEM 5-5 ___, Continued

ACCOUNT   *Accounts Payable*   ACCOUNT NO.   *21*

DATE		ITEM	POST. REF.	DEBIT	CREDIT	BALANCE	
						DEBIT	CREDIT

ACCOUNT   _____, *Capital*   ACCOUNT NO.   *31*

DATE		ITEM	POST. REF.	DEBIT	CREDIT	BALANCE	
						DEBIT	CREDIT

ACCOUNT   _____, *Drawing*   ACCOUNT NO.   *32*

DATE		ITEM	POST. REF.	DEBIT	CREDIT	BALANCE	
						DEBIT	CREDIT

ACCOUNT   *Fees Earned*   ACCOUNT NO.   *41*

DATE		ITEM	POST. REF.	DEBIT	CREDIT	BALANCE	
						DEBIT	CREDIT

PROBLEM 5-5 ___ , Continued

ACCOUNT   *Rent Revenue*   ACCOUNT NO.   *42*

DATE		ITEM	POST. REF.	DEBIT	CREDIT	BALANCE	
						DEBIT	CREDIT

ACCOUNT   *Driver Salaries Expense*   ACCOUNT NO.   *51*

DATE		ITEM	POST. REF.	DEBIT	CREDIT	BALANCE	
						DEBIT	CREDIT

ACCOUNT   *Maintenance Supplies Expense*   ACCOUNT NO.   *52*

DATE		ITEM	POST. REF.	DEBIT	CREDIT	BALANCE	
						DEBIT	CREDIT

ACCOUNT   *Fuel Expense*   ACCOUNT NO.   *53*

DATE		ITEM	POST. REF.	DEBIT	CREDIT	BALANCE	
						DEBIT	CREDIT

PROBLEM 5-5 ___, Continued

ACCOUNT   *Office Salaries Expense*   ACCOUNT NO.   *61*

DATE		ITEM	POST. REF.	DEBIT	CREDIT	BALANCE	
						DEBIT	CREDIT

ACCOUNT   *Rent Expense*   ACCOUNT NO.   *62*

DATE		ITEM	POST. REF.	DEBIT	CREDIT	BALANCE	
						DEBIT	CREDIT

ACCOUNT   *Advertising Expense*   ACCOUNT NO.   *63*

DATE		ITEM	POST. REF.	DEBIT	CREDIT	BALANCE	
						DEBIT	CREDIT

ACCOUNT   *Miscellaneous Administrative Expense*   ACCOUNT NO.   *64*

DATE		ITEM	POST. REF.	DEBIT	CREDIT	BALANCE	
						DEBIT	CREDIT

PROBLEM 5-5____, Continued

2. and 4.

PURCHASES JOURNAL

DATE	ACCOUNT CREDITED	POST. REF.	ACCOUNTS PAYABLE CR.	MAINTENANCE SUPPLIES DR.	OFFICE SUPPLIES DR.	OTHER ACCOUNTS DR.		
						ACCOUNT	POST. REF.	AMOUNT
1									1
2									2
3									3
4									4
5									5
6									6
7									7
8									8
9									9
10									10
11									11
12									12
13									13
14									14
15									15
16									16
17									17
18									18
19									19
20									20
21									21
22									22
23									23

PROBLEM 5-5 ___, Continued

2. and 4.   **CASH RECEIPTS JOURNAL**   PAGE *31*

	DATE	ACCOUNT CREDITED	POST. REF.	OTHER ACCOUNTS CR.	ACCOUNTS REC. CR.	CASH DR.	
1							1
2							2
3							3
4							4
5							5
6							6
7							7
8							8
9							9
10							10
11							11
12							12
13							13
14							14
15							15
16							16

2. and 4.   **REVENUE JOURNAL**   PAGE *35*

	DATE	INVOICE NO.	ACCOUNT DEBITED	POST. REF.	ACCTS. REC. DR. FEES EARNED CR.	
1						1
2						2
3						3
4						4
5						5
6						6
7						7
8						8
9						9
10						10
11						11
12						12
13						13
14						14

PROBLEM 5-5 ___ , Continued

2. and 4.   **CASH PAYMENTS JOURNAL**   PAGE *34*

	DATE	CK. NO.	ACCOUNT DEBITED	POST. REF.	OTHER ACCOUNTS DR.	ACCOUNTS PAYABLE DR.	CASH CR.	
1								1
2								2
3								3
4								4
5								5
6								6
7								7
8								8
9								9
10								10
11								11
12								12
13								13
14								14
15								15
16								16
17								17
18								18
19								19

3.   **JOURNAL**   PAGE *1*

	DATE	DESCRIPTION	POST. REF.	DEBIT	CREDIT	
1						1
2						2
3						3
4						4
5						5
6						6
7						7
8						8
9						9
10						10
11						11

PROBLEM 5-5 ___ , Concluded

5.

	Unadjusted Trial Balance	

This Page Not Used.

EXERCISE 6-1

a. _____

b. _____

c. _____

_____

EXERCISE 6-2

_____

EXERCISE 6-3

a. Net sales: _____

b. Gross profit: _____

c. _____

EXERCISE 6-4

1. Advertising expense: _____

2. Depreciation expense on store equipment: _____

3. Insurance expense on office equipment: _____

4. Interest expense on notes payable: _____

5. Rent expense on office building: _____

6. Salaries of office personnel: _____

7. Salary of sales manager: _____

8. Sales supplies used: _____

EXERCISE 6-5

	Income Statement		

EXERCISE 6-6

EXERCISE 6-6, Concluded
(Optional)

	Income Statement			

EXERCISE 6-7

Sales	$300,000	$600,000	$850,000	(g) $_____
Sales returns and allowances	(a) _____	30,000	(e) _____	10,000
Sales discounts	20,000	18,000	70,000	25,000
Net sales	250,000	(c) _____	775,000	(h) _____
Cost of merchandise sold	(b) _____	330,000	(f) _____	400,000
Gross profit	100,000	(d) _____	300,000	115,000

EXERCISE 6-8

a. _____

	Income Statement		

b. _____

_____

EXERCISE 6-9

Balance Sheet Accounts	
Acct #	Account Name

Income Statement Accounts	
Acct #	Account Name

EXERCISE 6-10

JOURNAL

	DATE		DESCRIPTION	POST. REF.	DEBIT	CREDIT	
1							1
2							2
3							3
4							4
5							5
6							6
7							7
8							8
9							9
10							10
11							11
12							12
13							13
14							14
15							15
16							16
17							17
18							18
19							19
20							20
21							21
22							22
23							23
24							24
25							25
26							26
27							27
28							28
29							29
30							30
31							31
32							32
33							33
34							34
35							35
36							36

EXERCISE 6-11

_____

_____

_____

_____

_____

_____

_____

_____

_____

_____

_____

EXERCISE 6-12

a. _____

b.

JOURNAL

PAGE

	DATE	DESCRIPTION	POST. REF.	DEBIT	CREDIT	
1						1
2						2
3						3
4						4
5						5
6						6

EXERCISE 6-13

(1) _____

_____

(2) _____

_____

(3) _____

_____

(4) _____

_____

(5) _____

_____

EXERCISE 6-14

a. Amount of the sale: _____

b. Amount debited to Accounts Receivable: _____

c. Amount of the discount for early payment: _____

d. Amount due within the discount period: _____

EXERCISE 6-15

a. _____

_____

b. _____

EXERCISE 6-16

_____

_____

_____

_____

_____

_____

_____

_____

_____

EXERCISE 6-17

(1) _____

_____

_____

(2) _____

_____

_____

(3) _____

_____

_____

(4) _____

_____

_____

EXERCISE 6-18

JOURNAL   PAGE

	DATE	DESCRIPTION	POST. REF.	DEBIT	CREDIT	
1						1
2						2
3						3
4						4
5						5
6						6
7						7
8						8
9						9
10						10

EXERCISE 6-19

		JOURNAL			PAGE	
	DATE	DESCRIPTION	POST. REF.	DEBIT	CREDIT	
1						1
2						2
3						3
4						4
5						5
6						6
7						7
8						8
9						9
10						10
11						11
12						12
13						13
14						14
15						15
16						16

EXERCISE 6-20

	Merchandise	Freight Paid by Seller		Returns and Allowances	Amount to be Paid in Full
a.	$36,000	—	FOB destination, n/30	$1,000	$ _____
b.	10,000	$375	FOB shipping point, 2/10, n/30	1,200	$ _____
c.	$8,250	—	FOB shipping point, 1/10, n/30	$750	$ _____
d.	4,000	200	FOB shipping point, 2/10, n/30	500	$ _____
e.	-8,500	—	FOB destination, 1/10, n/30	—	$ _____

EXERCISE 6-21

a. _____

b. _____

c. _____

d. _____

EXERCISE 6-22

JOURNAL   PAGE

	DATE		DESCRIPTION	POST. REF.	DEBIT	CREDIT	
1							1
2							2
3							3
4							4
5							5
6							6
7							7
8							8
9							9
10							10
11							11
12							12

EXERCISE 6-23

	DATE		DESCRIPTION	POST. REF.	DEBIT	CREDIT	
1							1
2							2
3							3
4							4
5							5
6							6
7							7
8							8
9							9
10							10
11							11
12							12
13							13
14							14
15							15
16							16
17							17
18							18

JOURNAL   PAGE

EXERCISE 6-24

	DATE		DESCRIPTION	POST. REF.	DEBIT	CREDIT	
1							1
2							2
3							3
4							4
5							5
6							6
7							7
8							8
9							9
10							10
11							11
12							12

JOURNAL   PAGE

EXERCISE 6-25

		Debit	Credit
a.	Cost of Merchandise Sold	_____	_____
b.	Delivery Expense	_____	_____
c.	Merchandise Inventory...........................	_____	_____
d.	Sales..	_____	_____
e.	Sales Discounts..................................	_____	_____
f.	Sales Returns and Allowances	_____	_____
g.	Sales Tax Payable	_____	_____

EXERCISE 6-26

JOURNAL   PAGE

	DATE	DESCRIPTION	POST. REF.	DEBIT	CREDIT	
1						1
2						2
3						3
4						4
5						5
6						6

EXERCISE 6-27

a. Accounts Payable: _____

b. Advertising Expense: _____

c. Cost of Merchandise Sold: _____

d. Merchandise Inventory: _____

e. Sales: _____

f. Sales Discounts: _____

g. Sales Returns and Allowances: _____

h. Supplies: _____

i. Supplies Expense: _____

j. Tyler Royce, Drawing: _____

k. Wages Payable: _____

EXERCISE 6-28

JOURNAL   PAGE

	DATE	DESCRIPTION	POST. REF.	DEBIT	CREDIT	
1						1
2						2
3						3
4						4
5						5
6						6
7						7
8						8
9						9
10						10
11						11
12						12
13						13
14						14
15						15
16						16
17						17
18						18
19						19
20						20
21						21
22						22
23						23

EXERCISE 6-29

JOURNAL   PAGE

	DATE		DESCRIPTION	POST. REF.	DEBIT	CREDIT	
1							1
2							2
3							3
4							4
5							5
6							6
7							7
8							8
9							9
10							10
11							11
12							12
13							13
14							14
15							15
16							16
17							17

EXERCISE 6-30

a. 2009: _____

    2008: _____

b. _____

_____

_____

_____

_____

_____

_____

_____

_____

EXERCISE 6-31

a. _____

b. _____

_____

_____

_____

_____

_____

_____

_____

_____

_____

_____

_____

APPENDIX EXERCISE 6-32

a. Purchases − (X + Y) = Net purchases

_____

b. Net purchases + X = Cost of merchandise purchased

_____

c. Merchandise inventory (beginning) + Cost of merchandise purchased = X

_____

d. Merchandise available for sale − X = Cost of merchandise sold

_____

APPENDIX EXERCISE 6-33

a.

b. _____

c. _____

APPENDIX EXERCISE 6-34

APPENDIX EXERCISE 6-35

APPENDIX EXERCISE 6-36

(Optional)

APPENDIX EXERCISE 6-37

Account	Increase	Decrease	Normal Balance
Purchases	(a) _____	credit	(b) _____
Purchase Discounts	(c) _____	debit	credit
Purchase Returns and Allowances	(d) _____	debit	(e) _____
Freight-In	(f) _____	(g) _____	debit

APPENDIX EXERCISE 6-38

JOURNAL

	DATE	DESCRIPTION	POST. REF.	DEBIT	CREDIT	
1						1
2						2
3						3
4						4
5						5
6						6
7						7
8						8
9						9
10						10
11						11
12						12
13						13
14						14
15						15
16						16
17						17
18						18
19						19
20						20
21						21
22						22
23						23
24						24
25						25

APPENDIX EXERCISE 6-39

JOURNAL

	DATE		DESCRIPTION	POST. REF.	DEBIT	CREDIT	
1							1
2							2
3							3
4							4
5							5
6							6
7							7
8							8
9							9
10							10
11							11
12							12
13							13
14							14
15							15
16							16
17							17
18							18
19							19
20							20
21							21
22							22
23							23
24							24
25							25
26							26
27							27

APPENDIX EXERCISE 6-40

JOURNAL

	DATE		DESCRIPTION	POST. REF.	DEBIT	CREDIT	
1							1
2							2
3							3
4							4
5							5
6							6
7							7
8							8
9							9
10							10
11							11
12							12
13							13
14							14
15							15
16							16
17							17
18							18
19							19
20							20
21							21
22							22
23							23
24							24
25							25

This Page Not Used.

PROBLEM 6-1 ___

1.

	Income Statement			

PROBLEM 6-1 ___, Continued

2.

Statement of Owner's Equity		

PROBLEM 6-1 ___ , Continued

3.

	Balance Sheet			

PROBLEM 6-1 ___, Concluded

4. a. _____

_____

_____

_____

_____

_____

_____

_____

_____

_____

_____

_____

_____

_____

_____

_____

_____

_____

b. _____

_____

_____

_____

_____

_____

_____

_____

_____

_____

_____

_____

_____

_____

_____

_____

_____

_____

_____

PROBLEM 6-2 ___

1.

Income Statement		

2.

Statement of Owner's Equity		

Name _____

PROBLEM 6-2 ____, Continued

3.

Balance Sheet

PROBLEM 6-2 ___, Concluded

4.

JOURNAL PAGE

	DATE		DESCRIPTION	POST. REF.	DEBIT	CREDIT	
1							1
2							2
3							3
4							4
5							5
6							6
7							7
8							8
9							9
10							10
11							11
12							12
13							13
14							14
15							15
16							16
17							17
18							18
19							19
20							20
21							21
22							22
23							23
24							24
25							25
26							26
27							27
28							28
29							29
30							30
31							31
32							32
33							33
34							34
35							35
36							36

This Page Not Used.

PROBLEM 6-3 ___

JOURNAL

	DATE		DESCRIPTION	POST. REF.	DEBIT	CREDIT	
1							1
2							2
3							3
4							4
5							5
6							6
7							7
8							8
9							9
10							10
11							11
12							12
13							13
14							14
15							15
16							16
17							17
18							18
19							19
20							20
21							21
22							22
23							23
24							24
25							25
26							26
27							27
28							28
29							29
30							30
31							31
32							32
33							33
34							34
35							35
36							36

PROBLEM 6-3 ___, Concluded

JOURNAL   PAGE

	DATE		DESCRIPTION	POST. REF.	DEBIT	CREDIT	
1							1
2							2
3							3
4							4
5							5
6							6
7							7
8							8
9							9
10							10
11							11
12							12
13							13
14							14
15							15
16							16
17							17
18							18
19							19
20							20
21							21
22							22
23							23
24							24
25							25
26							26
27							27
28							28
29							29
30							30
31							31
32							32
33							33
34							34
35							35
36							36

PROBLEM 6-4 ___

JOURNAL   PAGE

	DATE	DESCRIPTION	POST. REF.	DEBIT	CREDIT	
1						1
2						2
3						3
4						4
5						5
6						6
7						7
8						8
9						9
10						10
11						11
12						12
13						13
14						14
15						15
16						16
17						17
18						18
19						19
20						20
21						21
22						22
23						23
24						24
25						25
26						26
27						27
28						28
29						29
30						30
31						31
32						32
33						33
34						34
35						35
36						36

PROBLEM 6- 4___, Concluded

	DATE		DESCRIPTION	POST. REF.	DEBIT	CREDIT	
1							1
2							2
3							3
4							4
5							5
6							6
7							7
8							8
9							9
10							10
11							11
12							12
13							13
14							14
15							15
16							16
17							17
18							18
19							19
20							20
21							21
22							22
23							23
24							24
25							25
26							26
27							27
28							28
29							29
30							30
31							31
32							32
33							33
34							34
35							35
36							36

JOURNAL   PAGE

PROBLEM 6-5 ___

	JOURNAL				PAGE

	DATE	DESCRIPTION	POST. REF.	DEBIT	CREDIT	
1						1
2						2
3						3
4						4
5						5
6						6
7						7
8						8
9						9
10						10
11						11
12						12
13						13
14						14
15						15
16						16
17						17
18						18
19						19
20						20
21						21
22						22
23						23
24						24
25						25
26						26
27						27
28						28
29						29
30						30
31						31
32						32
33						33
34						34
35						35
36						36

PROBLEM 6-5___, Concluded

JOURNAL   PAGE

	DATE		DESCRIPTION	POST. REF.	DEBIT	CREDIT	
1							1
2							2
3							3
4							4
5							5
6							6
7							7
8							8
9							9
10							10
11							11
12							12
13							13
14							14
15							15
16							16
17							17
18							18
19							19
20							20
21							21
22							22
23							23
24							24
25							25
26							26
27							27
28							28
29							29
30							30
31							31
32							32
33							33
34							34
35							35
36							36

PROBLEM 6-6 ___

1.

JOURNAL   PAGE

	DATE		DESCRIPTION	POST. REF.	DEBIT	CREDIT	
1							1
2							2
3							3
4							4
5							5
6							6
7							7
8							8
9							9
10							10
11							11
12							12
13							13
14							14
15							15
16							16
17							17
18							18
19							19
20							20
21							21
22							22
23							23
24							24
25							25
26							26
27							27
28							28
29							29
30							30
31							31
32							32
33							33
34							34
35							35
36							36

PROBLEM 6-6 ___ , Concluded

2.

JOURNAL   PAGE

	DATE		DESCRIPTION	POST. REF.	DEBIT	CREDIT	
1							1
2							2
3							3
4							4
5							5
6							6
7							7
8							8
9							9
10							10
11							11
12							12
13							13
14							14
15							15
16							16
17							17
18							18
19							19
20							20
21							21
22							22
23							23
24							24
25							25
26							26
27							27
28							28
29							29
30							30
31							31
32							32
33							33
34							34
35							35
36							36

APPENDIX PROBLEM 6-7 ___

JOURNAL   PAGE

	DATE	DESCRIPTION	POST. REF.	DEBIT	CREDIT	
1						1
2						2
3						3
4						4
5						5
6						6
7						7
8						8
9						9
10						10
11						11
12						12
13						13
14						14
15						15
16						16
17						17
18						18
19						19
20						20
21						21
22						22
23						23
24						24
25						25
26						26
27						27
28						28
29						29
30						30
31						31
32						32
33						33
34						34
35						35
36						36

APPENDIX PROBLEM 6-7 ___, Concluded

JOURNAL

	DATE	DESCRIPTION	POST. REF.	DEBIT	CREDIT	
1						1
2						2
3						3
4						4
5						5
6						6
7						7
8						8
9						9
10						10
11						11
12						12
13						13
14						14
15						15
16						16
17						17
18						18
19						19
20						20
21						21
22						22
23						23
24						24
25						25
26						26
27						27
28						28
29						29
30						30
31						31
32						32
33						33
34						34
35						35
36						36

APPENDIX PROBLEM 6-8 ___

JOURNAL   PAGE

	DATE	DESCRIPTION	POST. REF.	DEBIT	CREDIT	
1						1
2						2
3						3
4						4
5						5
6						6
7						7
8						8
9						9
10						10
11						11
12						12
13						13
14						14
15						15
16						16
17						17
18						18
19						19
20						20
21						21
22						22
23						23
24						24
25						25
26						26
27						27
28						28
29						29
30						30
31						31
32						32
33						33
34						34
35						35
36						36

APPENDIX PROBLEM 6-8 ___, Concluded

JOURNAL

PAGE

	DATE	DESCRIPTION	POST. REF.	DEBIT	CREDIT	
1						1
2						2
3						3
4						4
5						5
6						6
7						7
8						8
9						9
10						10
11						11
12						12
13						13
14						14
15						15
16						16
17						17
18						18
19						19
20						20
21						21
22						22
23						23
24						24
25						25
26						26
27						27
28						28
29						29
30						30
31						31
32						32
33						33
34						34
35						35
36						36

APPENDIX PROBLEM 6-9 ___

1.

| | | **JOURNAL** | | | PAGE |

	DATE	DESCRIPTION	POST. REF.	DEBIT	CREDIT	
1						1
2						2
3						3
4						4
5						5
6						6
7						7
8						8
9						9
10						10
11						11
12						12
13						13
14						14
15						15
16						16
17						17
18						18
19						19
20						20
21						21
22						22
23						23
24						24
25						25
26						26
27						27
28						28
29						29
30						30
31						31
32						32
33						33
34						34
35						35
36						36

APPENDIX PROBLEM 6-9 ___, Concluded

2.

JOURNAL

PAGE

	DATE		DESCRIPTION	POST. REF.	DEBIT	CREDIT	
1							1
2							2
3							3
4							4
5							5
6							6
7							7
8							8
9							9
10							10
11							11
12							12
13							13
14							14
15							15
16							16
17							17
18							18
19							19
20							20
21							21
22							22
23							23
24							24
25							25
26							26
27							27
28							28
29							29
30							30
31							31
32							32
33							33
34							34
35							35
36							36

APPENDIX PROBLEM 6-10 ___

1.

_____

_____

_____

2.

Income Statement

APPENDIX PROBLEM 6-10 ___, Continued

2.

Income Statement (Continued)			

APPENDIX PROBLEM 6-10 ___, Concluded

3.

JOURNAL   PAGE

	DATE		DESCRIPTION	POST. REF.	DEBIT	CREDIT	
1							1
2							2
3							3
4							4
5							5
6							6
7							7
8							8
9							9
10							10
11							11
12							12
13							13
14							14
15							15
16							16
17							17
18							18
19							19
20							20
21							21
22							22
23							23
24							24
25							25
26							26
27							27
28							28
29							29
30							30
31							31

4. _____

This Page Not Used.

COMPREHENSIVE PROBLEM 2

1., 2., 6., and 9.

ACCOUNT *Cash*   ACCOUNT NO. *110*

DATE		ITEM	POST. REF.	DEBIT	CREDIT	BALANCE	
						DEBIT	CREDIT

COMPREHENSIVE PROBLEM 2, Continued

ACCOUNT   *Accounts Receivable*   ACCOUNT NO.   *112*

DATE		ITEM	POST. REF.	DEBIT	CREDIT	BALANCE	
						DEBIT	CREDIT

ACCOUNT   *Merchandise Inventory*   ACCOUNT NO.   *115*

DATE		ITEM	POST. REF.	DEBIT	CREDIT	BALANCE	
						DEBIT	CREDIT

COMPREHENSIVE PROBLEM 2, Continued

ACCOUNT *Prepaid Insurance*   ACCOUNT NO. 116

DATE		ITEM	POST. REF.	DEBIT	CREDIT	BALANCE	
						DEBIT	CREDIT

ACCOUNT *Store Supplies*   ACCOUNT NO. 117

DATE		ITEM	POST. REF.	DEBIT	CREDIT	BALANCE	
						DEBIT	CREDIT

ACCOUNT *Store Equipment*   ACCOUNT NO. 123

DATE		ITEM	POST. REF.	DEBIT	CREDIT	BALANCE	
						DEBIT	CREDIT

ACCOUNT *Accumulated Depreciation—Store Equipment*   ACCOUNT NO. 124

DATE		ITEM	POST. REF.	DEBIT	CREDIT	BALANCE	
						DEBIT	CREDIT

COMPREHENSIVE PROBLEM 2, Continued

ACCOUNT   *Accounts Payable*   ACCOUNT NO.   *210*

DATE		ITEM	POST. REF.	DEBIT	CREDIT	BALANCE	
						DEBIT	CREDIT

ACCOUNT   *Salaries Payable*   ACCOUNT NO.   *211*

DATE		ITEM	POST. REF.	DEBIT	CREDIT	BALANCE	
						DEBIT	CREDIT

ACCOUNT   *Kevin Gilmour, Capital*   ACCOUNT NO.   *310*

DATE		ITEM	POST. REF.	DEBIT	CREDIT	BALANCE	
						DEBIT	CREDIT

ACCOUNT   *Kevin Gilmour, Drawing*   ACCOUNT NO.   *311*

DATE		ITEM	POST. REF.	DEBIT	CREDIT	BALANCE	
						DEBIT	CREDIT

COMPREHENSIVE PROBLEM 2, Continued

ACCOUNT *Income Summary*   ACCOUNT NO. *312*

DATE		ITEM	POST. REF.	DEBIT	CREDIT	BALANCE	
						DEBIT	CREDIT

ACCOUNT *Sales*   ACCOUNT NO. *410*

DATE		ITEM	POST. REF.	DEBIT	CREDIT	BALANCE	
						DEBIT	CREDIT

ACCOUNT *Sales Returns and Allowances*   ACCOUNT NO. *411*

DATE		ITEM	POST. REF.	DEBIT	CREDIT	BALANCE	
						DEBIT	CREDIT

COMPREHENSIVE PROBLEM 2, Continued

ACCOUNT   *Sales Discounts*   ACCOUNT NO.   412

DATE		ITEM	POST. REF.	DEBIT	CREDIT	BALANCE	
						DEBIT	CREDIT

ACCOUNT   *Cost of Merchandise Sold*   ACCOUNT NO.   510

DATE		ITEM	POST. REF.	DEBIT	CREDIT	BALANCE	
						DEBIT	CREDIT

ACCOUNT   *Sales Salaries Expense*   ACCOUNT NO.   520

DATE		ITEM	POST. REF.	DEBIT	CREDIT	BALANCE	
						DEBIT	CREDIT

COMPREHENSIVE PROBLEM 2, Continued

ACCOUNT   *Advertising Expense*   ACCOUNT NO.   521

DATE		ITEM	POST. REF.	DEBIT	CREDIT	BALANCE DEBIT	CREDIT

ACCOUNT   *Depreciation Expense*   ACCOUNT NO.   522

DATE		ITEM	POST. REF.	DEBIT	CREDIT	BALANCE DEBIT	CREDIT

ACCOUNT   *Store Supplies Expense*   ACCOUNT NO.   523

DATE		ITEM	POST. REF.	DEBIT	CREDIT	BALANCE DEBIT	CREDIT

ACCOUNT   *Miscellaneous Selling Expense*   ACCOUNT NO.   529

DATE		ITEM	POST. REF.	DEBIT	CREDIT	BALANCE DEBIT	CREDIT

COMPREHENSIVE PROBLEM 2, Continued

ACCOUNT   *Office Salaries Expense*   ACCOUNT NO.   *530*

DATE	ITEM	POST. REF.	DEBIT	CREDIT	BALANCE	
					DEBIT	CREDIT

ACCOUNT   *Rent Expense*   ACCOUNT NO.   *531*

DATE	ITEM	POST. REF.	DEBIT	CREDIT	BALANCE	
					DEBIT	CREDIT

ACCOUNT   *Insurance Expense*   ACCOUNT NO.   *532*

DATE	ITEM	POST. REF.	DEBIT	CREDIT	BALANCE	
					DEBIT	CREDIT

ACCOUNT   *Miscellaneous Administrative Expense*   ACCOUNT NO.   *539*

DATE	ITEM	POST. REF.	DEBIT	CREDIT	BALANCE	
					DEBIT	CREDIT

COMPREHENSIVE PROBLEM 2, Continued

1. and 2.

JOURNAL   PAGE *20*

	DATE		DESCRIPTION	POST. REF.	DEBIT	CREDIT	
1							1
2							2
3							3
4							4
5							5
6							6
7							7
8							8
9							9
10							10
11							11
12							12
13							13
14							14
15							15
16							16
17							17
18							18
19							19
20							20
21							21
22							22
23							23
24							24
25							25
26							26
27							27
28							28
29							29
30							30
31							31
32							32
33							33
34							34
35							35
36							36

COMPREHENSIVE PROBLEM 2, Continued

JOURNAL

PAGE *20*
continued

	DATE		DESCRIPTION	POST. REF.	DEBIT	CREDIT	
1							1
2							2
3							3
4							4
5							5
6							6
7							7
8							8
9							9
10							10
11							11
12							12
13							13
14							14
15							15

JOURNAL

PAGE *21*

	DATE		DESCRIPTION	POST. REF.	DEBIT	CREDIT	
1							1
2							2
3							3
4							4
5							5
6							6
7							7
8							8
9							9
10							10
11							11
12							12
13							13
14							14
15							15
16							16

COMPREHENSIVE PROBLEM 2, Continued

JOURNAL

	DATE		DESCRIPTION	POST. REF.	DEBIT	CREDIT	
1							1
2							2
3							3
4							4
5							5
6							6
7							7
8							8
9							9
10							10
11							11
12							12
13							13
14							14
15							15
16							16
17							17
18							18
19							19
20							20
21							21
22							22
23							23
24							24
25							25
26							26
27							27
28							28
29							29
30							30
31							31
32							32
33							33
34							34

COMPREHENSIVE PROBLEM 2, Continued

3.

Unadjusted Trial Balance		

COMPREHENSIVE PROBLEM 2, Continued

4. and 6.

JOURNAL

PAGE 22

	DATE		DESCRIPTION	POST. REF.	DEBIT	CREDIT	
1			*Adjusting Entries*				1
2							2
3							3
4							4
5							5
6							6
7							7
8							8
9							9
10							10
11							11
12							12
13							13
14							14
15							15
16							16
17							17
18							18
19							19
20							20
21							21
22							22
23							23
24							24
25							25
26							26
27							27
28							28
29							29
30							30
31							31
32							32
33							33
34							34
35							35
36							36

COMPREHENSIVE PROBLEM 2, Continued

7.

Adjusted Trial Balance		

COMPREHENSIVE PROBLEM 2, Continued

8.

Income Statement			

COMPREHENSIVE PROBLEM 2, Continued

Statement of Owner's Equity		

COMPREHENSIVE PROBLEM 2, Continued

	Balance Sheet		

COMPREHENSIVE PROBLEM 2, Continued

9.

| | JOURNAL | | | PAGE 23 |

	DATE		DESCRIPTION	POST. REF.	DEBIT	CREDIT	
1			*Closing Entries*				1
2							2
3							3
4							4
5							5
6							6
7							7
8							8
9							9
10							10
11							11
12							12
13							13
14							14
15							15
16							16
17							17
18							18
19							19
20							20
21							21
22							22
23							23
24							24
25							25
26							26
27							27
28							28
29							29
30							30
31							31
32							32
33							33
34							34
35							35
36							36

COMPREHENSIVE PROBLEM 2, Continued

10.

Post-Closing Trial Balance		

Name _____

COMPREHENSIVE PROBLEM 2, Concluded

5. **Optional** _This work sheet is applicable only if the end-of-period spreadsheet (work sheet) is used._

End-of-Period Spreadsheet (Work Sheet)

	Unadjusted Trial Balance		Adjustments		Adjusted Trial Balance		Income Statement		Balance Sheet	
Account Title	Dr.	Cr.	Dr.	Cr.	Dr.	Cr.	Dr.	Cr.	Dr.	Cr.

EXERCISE 7-1

_____
_____
_____
_____
_____
_____
_____
_____
_____
_____
_____
_____
_____
_____

EXERCISE 7-2

a. _____
_____
_____
_____
_____
_____

b. _____
_____
_____
_____
_____

c. _____
_____
_____
_____
_____

EXERCISE 7-3

a.

Portable Video Players

Date	Purchases			Cost of Merchandise Sold			Inventory		
	Quantity	Unit Cost	Total Cost	Quantity	Unit Cost	Total Cost	Quantity	Unit Cost	Total Cost

b.

EXERCISE 7-4

Portable Video Players

Date	Purchases			Cost of Merchandise Sold			Inventory		
	Quantity	Unit Cost	Total Cost	Quantity	Unit Cost	Total Cost	Quantity	Unit Cost	Total Cost

EXERCISE 7-5

a.

Prepaid Cell Phones

Date	Purchases			Cost of Merchandise Sold			Inventory		
	Quantity	Unit Cost	Total Cost	Quantity	Unit Cost	Total Cost	Quantity	Unit Cost	Total Cost

b. _____

EXERCISE 7-6

Prepaid Cell Phones

Date	Purchases			Cost of Merchandise Sold			Inventory		
	Quantity	Unit Cost	Total Cost	Quantity	Unit Cost	Total Cost	Quantity	Unit Cost	Total Cost

EXERCISE 7-7

a. FIFO: _____

b. LIFO: _____

EXERCISE 7-8

a. First-in, first-out method: _____

_____

b. Last-in, first-out method: _____

_____

c. Average cost method: _____

_____

_____

_____

_____

_____

_____

_____

EXERCISE 7-9

	Cost	
Inventory Method	**Merchandise Inventory**	**Merchandise Sold**
a. First-in, first-out..............	_____	_____
b. Last-in, first-out..............	_____	_____
c. Average cost..................	_____	_____

Supporting calculations:

_____

_____

_____

_____

_____

_____

_____

_____

_____

_____

_____

_____

_____

_____

EXERCISE 7-10

a.

1.FIFO inventory _____ LIFO inventory

2. FIFO cost of goods sold _____ LIFO cost of goods sold

3. FIFO net income _____ LIFO net income

4. FIFO income tax _____ LIFO income tax

b. _____

_____

_____

_____

_____

_____

_____

_____

_____

_____

_____

_____

EXERCISE 7-11

	A	B	C	D	E	F	G
1			Unit	Unit		Total	
2		Inventory	Cost	Market			Lower
3	Commodity	Quantity	Price	Price	Cost	Market	of C or M
4	AL65	40	$ 28	$ 30			
5	CA22	50	70	65			
6	LA98	110	6	5			
7	SC16	30	40	30			
8	UT28	75	60	62			
9	Total						

EXERCISE 7-12

_____
_____
_____
_____
_____

EXERCISE 7-13

a.

	Balance Sheet
Merchandise inventory	_____
Current assets	_____
Total assets	_____
Owner's equity	_____

b.

	Income Statement
Cost of merchandise sold	_____
Gross profit	_____
Net income	_____

c.

	Income Statement
Cost of merchandise sold	_____
Gross profit	_____
Net income	_____

d. _____
_____
_____

EXERCISE 7-14

a.

	Balance Sheet
Merchandise inventory	_____
Current assets	_____
Total assets	_____
Owner's equity	_____

b.

	Income Statement
Cost of merchandise sold	_____
Gross profit	_____
Net income	_____

EXERCISE 7-14, Concluded

c.   **Income Statement**

Cost of merchandise sold ....   _____

Gross profit ....   _____

Net income...   _____

d. _____

_____

_____

EXERCISE 7-15

_____

_____

_____

_____

_____

_____

_____

_____

_____

_____

_____

_____

_____

_____

_____

EXERCISE 7-16

a. Apple: _____

American Greetings: _____

b. _____

_____

_____

_____

_____

_____

_____

_____

EXERCISE 7-17

a. Number of Days' Sales in Inventory =

_____

Kroger: _____

_____

Safeway: _____

_____

Winn-Dixie: _____

_____

Inventory Turnover =

_____

Kroger: _____

_____

Safeway: _____

_____

Winn-Dixie: _____

_____

b. _____

_____

_____

_____

_____

_____

EXERCISE 7-17, Concluded

c. _____

APPENDIX EXERCISE 7-18

APPENDIX EXERCISE 7-19

APPENDIX EXERCISE 7-20

APPENDIX EXERCISE 7-21

	A	B	C
1		Cost	Retail
2			
3			
4			
5			
6			
7			
8			

APPENDIX EXERCISE 7-22

a.

	A	B	C
1		Cost	Retail
2			
3			
4			
5			
6			
7			
8			

b.

_____

_____

_____

_____

APPENDIX EXERCISE 7-23

APPENDIX EXERCISE 7-24

This Page Not Used.

Name _____

Chapter 7

PROBLEM 7-1 ___

1.

Date	Purchases			Cost of Merchandise Sold			Inventory		
	Quantity	Unit Cost	Total Cost	Quantity	Unit Cost	Total Cost	Quantity	Unit Cost	Total Cost

PROBLEM 7-1 ___ , Concluded

2.

JOURNAL

PAGE

	DATE		DESCRIPTION	POST. REF.	DEBIT	CREDIT	
1							1
2							2
3							3
4							4
5							5
6							6
7							7
8							8
9							9
10							10

3. _____

4. _____

5. _____
_____
_____

PROBLEM 7-2 ___

1.

Date	Purchases			Cost of Merchandise Sold			Inventory		
	Quantity	Unit Cost	Total Cost	Quantity	Unit Cost	Total Cost	Quantity	Unit Cost	Total Cost

PROBLEM 7-2 ___, Concluded

2.

_____

_____

_____

3.

_____

PROBLEM 7-3 ___

1.   First-In, First-Out Method

Model	Quantity	Unit Cost	Total Cost

2.   Last-In, First-Out Method

Model	Quantity	Unit Cost	Total Cost

PROBLEM 7-3 ___ , Concluded

3.   **Average Cost Method**

Model	Quantity	Unit Cost	Total Cost

Computations of unit costs:

_____

_____

_____

_____

_____

_____

_____

_____

4. a. _____

_____

_____

_____

_____

_____

_____

_____

b. _____

_____

_____

_____

PROBLEM 7-4 ___

	A	B	C	D	E	F	G	H
1				Inventory Sheet December 31, 2012				
2				Unit	Unit		Total	
3		Inventory		Cost	Market			Lower
4	Description	Quantity		Price	Price	Cost	Market	of C or M
5	Alpha	38	30	$ 60	$ 57	$1,800	$1,710	
6			8	59		472	456	
7						2,272	2,166	$ 2,166
8	Beta	20			180			
9	Charlie	30			125			
10								
11								
12	Echo	125			26			
13	Frank	18			550			
14								
15								
16	George	75			17			
17	Killo	5			390			
18	Quebec	375			6			
19	Romeo	90			18			
20								
21								
22	Sierra	6			235			
23								
24								
25	Whiskey	140			20			
26								
27								
28	X-Ray	15			745			
29								
30								
31	Total							
32								
33								

This Page Not Used.

APPENDIX PROBLEM 7-5 ___

1.

	A	B	C
1			
2		Cost	Retail
3			
4			
5			
6			
7			
8			
9			
10			
11			
12			

2.

	A	B	C
1			
2	a.	Cost	Retail
3			
4			
5			
6			
7			
8			
9			
10			
11			
12			
13	b.		
14			
15			
16			
17			

This Page Not Used.

EXERCISE 8-1

EXERCISE 8-2

a. _____
_____
_____
_____

b. _____
_____
_____
_____
_____

c. _____
_____
_____
_____
_____
_____
_____
_____
_____

EXERCISE 8-3

a. _____
_____
_____
_____

b. _____
_____
_____
_____
_____
_____

EXERCISE 8-3, Concluded

c. _____

_____

_____

_____

_____

_____

_____

_____

_____

_____

_____

_____

_____

_____

_____

_____

_____

_____

_____

_____

_____

_____

_____

d. _____

_____

_____

_____

_____

_____

_____

_____

_____

EXERCISE 8-4

EXERCISE 8-5

EXERCISE 8-6

_____

_____

_____

_____

_____

_____

_____

_____

_____

_____

_____

_____

_____

_____

_____

_____

_____

_____

_____

_____

EXERCISE 8-7

_____
_____
_____
_____
_____
_____
_____
_____
_____
_____
_____
_____
_____
_____
_____
_____
_____
_____
_____
_____
_____

EXERCISE 8-8

a. _____
_____
_____
_____
_____
_____
_____

b. _____
_____
_____
_____
_____
_____

EXERCISE 8-9

a. _____

_____

_____

_____

_____

_____

_____

b. _____

_____

_____

_____

_____

_____

_____

EXERCISE 8-10

_____

EXERCISE 8-11

a. _____

b. _____

EXERCISE 8-12

JOURNAL   PAGE

	DATE	DESCRIPTION	POST. REF.	DEBIT	CREDIT	
1						1
2						2
3						3
4						4
5						5
6						6
7						7
8						8
9						9
10						10
11						11
12						12
13						13
14						14

EXERCISE 8-13

JOURNAL   PAGE

	DATE	DESCRIPTION	POST. REF.	DEBIT	CREDIT	
1						1
2						2
3						3
4						4
5						5
6						6
7						7
8						8
9						9
10						10
11						11
12						12
13						13
14						14

EXERCISE 8-14

EXERCISE 8-15

_____
_____
_____
_____
_____
_____
_____
_____
_____
_____
_____
_____
_____
_____
_____
_____
_____
_____
_____
_____
_____

EXERCISE 8-16

a. Addition to the cash balance per bank: _____

b. Deduction from the cash balance per bank: _____

c. Addition to the cash balance per company's records: _____

d. Deduction from the cash balance per company's records: _____

EXERCISE 8-17

_____

EXERCISE 8-18

a. _____

Bank Reconciliation	

b. _____

c. _____

EXERCISE 8-19

	JOURNAL				PAGE	
	DATE	DESCRIPTION	POST. REF.	DEBIT	CREDIT	
1						1
2						2
3						3
4						4
5						5

EXERCISE 8-20

	JOURNAL				PAGE	
	DATE	DESCRIPTION	POST. REF.	DEBIT	CREDIT	
1						1
2						2
3						3
4						4

EXERCISE 8-21

a.

	Bank Reconciliation		

b. _____

EXERCISE 8-22

_____

_____

_____

_____

_____

_____

_____

EXERCISE 8-22, Concluded

_____
_____
_____
_____
_____

Optional

_____

Bank Reconciliation

EXERCISE 8-23

a. _____

b.

EXERCISE 8-24

a. and b.

	DATE		DESCRIPTION	POST. REF.	DEBIT	CREDIT	
1							1
2							2
3							3
4							4
5							5
6							6
7							7
8							8

JOURNAL   PAGE

EXERCISE 8-25

_____

_____

_____

_____

_____

_____

EXERCISE 8-26

a.

_____

_____

b.

_____

_____

_____

_____

_____

_____

EXERCISE 8-27

a.
_____

b.
_____

c.
_____
_____
_____
_____
_____
_____
_____

EXERCISE   8-28

a.
2008: _____
2007: _____
2006: _____

b.
2008: _____
2007: _____
2006: _____

c.
_____
_____
_____
_____
_____
_____
_____
_____
_____
_____

This Page Not Used.

PROBLEM 8-1 ___

This Page Not Used.

PROBLEM 8-2 ___

JOURNAL   PAGE

	DATE	DESCRIPTION	POST. REF.	DEBIT	CREDIT	
1						1
2						2
3						3
4						4
5						5
6						6
7						7
8						8
9						9
10						10
11						11
12						12
13						13
14						14
15						15
16						16
17						17
18						18
19						19
20						20
21						21
22						22
23						23
24						24
25						25
26						26
27						27
28						28
29						29
30						30
31						31
32						32
33						33
34						34
35						35
36						36

This Page Not Used.

PROBLEM 8-3 ___

1.

Bank Reconciliation		

2.

JOURNAL   PAGE

	DATE		DESCRIPTION	POST. REF.	DEBIT	CREDIT	
1							1
2							2
3							3
4							4
5							5
6							6
7							7

3. _____

394

This Page Not Used.

PROBLEM 8-4 ___

1.

	Bank Reconciliation		

PROBLEM 8-4 ___, Concluded

2.

	DATE		DESCRIPTION	POST. REF.	DEBIT	CREDIT	
1							1
2							2
3							3
4							4
5							5
6							6
7							7
8							8
9							9
10							10
11							11
12							12
13							13
14							14
15							15
16							16
17							17
18							18
19							19
20							20
21							21
22							22
23							23
24							24
25							25
26							26
27							27
28							28
29							29
30							30
31							31
32							32
33							33

JOURNAL   PAGE

3. _____

PROBLEM 8-5 ___

1.

	Bank Reconciliation		

PROBLEM 8-5 ___, Concluded

2.

<table>
<tr><td colspan="2">JOURNAL</td><td></td><td></td><td>PAGE</td></tr>
<tr><th colspan="2">DATE</th><th>DESCRIPTION</th><th>POST. REF.</th><th>DEBIT</th><th>CREDIT</th></tr>
<tr><td></td><td></td><td></td><td></td><td></td><td></td></tr>
<tr><td></td><td></td><td></td><td></td><td></td><td></td></tr>
<tr><td></td><td></td><td></td><td></td><td></td><td></td></tr>
<tr><td></td><td></td><td></td><td></td><td></td><td></td></tr>
<tr><td></td><td></td><td></td><td></td><td></td><td></td></tr>
<tr><td></td><td></td><td></td><td></td><td></td><td></td></tr>
<tr><td></td><td></td><td></td><td></td><td></td><td></td></tr>
<tr><td></td><td></td><td></td><td></td><td></td><td></td></tr>
<tr><td></td><td></td><td></td><td></td><td></td><td></td></tr>
<tr><td></td><td></td><td></td><td></td><td></td><td></td></tr>
<tr><td></td><td></td><td></td><td></td><td></td><td></td></tr>
<tr><td></td><td></td><td></td><td></td><td></td><td></td></tr>
<tr><td></td><td></td><td></td><td></td><td></td><td></td></tr>
<tr><td></td><td></td><td></td><td></td><td></td><td></td></tr>
<tr><td></td><td></td><td></td><td></td><td></td><td></td></tr>
<tr><td></td><td></td><td></td><td></td><td></td><td></td></tr>
<tr><td></td><td></td><td></td><td></td><td></td><td></td></tr>
<tr><td></td><td></td><td></td><td></td><td></td><td></td></tr>
<tr><td></td><td></td><td></td><td></td><td></td><td></td></tr>
<tr><td></td><td></td><td></td><td></td><td></td><td></td></tr>
<tr><td></td><td></td><td></td><td></td><td></td><td></td></tr>
<tr><td></td><td></td><td></td><td></td><td></td><td></td></tr>
<tr><td></td><td></td><td></td><td></td><td></td><td></td></tr>
<tr><td></td><td></td><td></td><td></td><td></td><td></td></tr>
</table>

3. _____

4.

_____

_____

_____

_____

_____

_____

EXERCISE 9-1

_____

_____

_____

_____

_____

_____

_____

EXERCISE 9-2

a. _____

_____

_____

b. _____

_____

_____

c. _____

_____

_____

_____

_____

_____

_____

_____

_____

EXERCISE 9-3

JOURNAL

	DATE	DESCRIPTION	POST. REF.	DEBIT	CREDIT	
1						1
2						2
3						3
4						4
5						5
6						6
7						7
8						8
9						9
10						10
11						11
12						12
13						13
14						14
15						15
16						16
17						17
18						18
19						19
20						20

EXERCISE 9-4

JOURNAL PAGE

	DATE		DESCRIPTION	POST. REF.	DEBIT	CREDIT	
1							1
2							2
3							3
4							4
5							5
6							6
7							7
8							8
9							9
10							10
11							11
12							12
13							13
14							14
15							15
16							16
17							17

EXERCISE 9-5

a.–b.

JOURNAL PAGE

	DATE		DESCRIPTION	POST. REF.	DEBIT	CREDIT	
1							1
2							2
3							3
4							4
5							5
6							6
7							7
8							8
9							9
10							10

EXERCISE 9-6

a. _____

b. _____

c. _____

b. _____

EXERCISE 9-7

Account	Due Date	Number of Days Past Due
Alpha Auto	May 15	
Best Auto	July 8	
Downtown Repair	March 18	
Lucky's Auto Repair	June 1	
Pit Stop Auto	June 3	
Sally's	April 12	
Trident Auto	May 31	
Washburn Repair & Tow	March 2	

EXERCISE 9-8

a.

Customer	Due Date	Number of Days Past Due
Beltran Industries	July 10	
Doodle Company	September 20	
La Corp Inc.	October 17	
VIP Sales Company	November 4	
We-Go Company	December 21	

EXERCISE 9-8, Concluded

b.

	A	B	C	D	E	F	G
1			Aging of Receivables Schedule				
2			November 30				
3					Days Past Due		
4	Customer	Balance	Not Past Due	1–30	31–60	61–90	Over 90
5	Able Brothers Inc.	3,000	3,000				
6	Accent Company	4,500		4,500			
21	Zumpano Company	5,000			5,000		
22	Subtotals	830,000	500,000	180,000	80,000	45,000	25,000
23							
24							
25							
26							
27							
28							

EXERCISE 9-9

	BALANCE	NOT PAST DUE	1–30	31–60	61–90	OVER 90
				DAYS PAST DUE		

EXERCISE 9-10

JOURNAL

	DATE		DESCRIPTION	POST. REF.	DEBIT	CREDIT	
1							1
2							2
3							3
4							4
5							5

EXERCISE 9-11

Age Interval	Balance	Estimated Uncollectible Accounts Percent	Amount
Not past due..	$600,000	¼%	$ _____
1–30 days past due............................	120,000	2	_____
31–60 days past due	60,000	3	_____
61–90 days past due..........................	45,000	10	_____
91–180 days past due........................	26,000	40	_____
Over 180 days past due......................	24,000	75	_____
Total..	$875,000		$ _____

EXERCISE 9-12

JOURNAL

	DATE		DESCRIPTION	POST. REF.	DEBIT	CREDIT	
1							1
2							2
3							3
4							4
5							5

EXERCISE 9-13

a.

	JOURNAL				PAGE

	DATE		DESCRIPTION	POST. REF.	DEBIT	CREDIT	
1							1
2							2
3							3
4							4
5							5
6							6
7							7
8							8
9							9
10							10
11							11
12							12
13							13
14							14
15							15
16							16
17							17
18							18
19							19
20							20
21							21
22							22
23							23
24							24
25							25
26							26
27							27
28							28
29							29
30							30
31							31
32							32
33							33
34							34
35							35
36							36

EXERCISE 9-13, Concluded

b.

JOURNAL PAGE

	DATE		DESCRIPTION	POST. REF.	DEBIT	CREDIT	
1							1
2							2
3							3
4							4
5							5
6							6
7							7
8							8
9							9
10							10
11							11
12							12
13							13
14							14
15							15
16							16
17							17
18							18
19							19
20							20
21							21
22							22
23							23
24							24

c.

EXERCISE 9-14

a.

	DATE		DESCRIPTION	POST. REF.	DEBIT	CREDIT	
1							1
2							2
3							3
4							4
5							5
6							6
7							7
8							8
9							9
10							10
11							11
12							12
13							13
14							14
15							15
16							16
17							17
18							18
19							19
20							20
21							21
22							22
23							23
24							24
25							25
26							26
27							27
28							28
29							29
30							30
31							31
32							32
33							33
34							34
35							35
36							36

EXERCISE 9-14, Continued

b.

JOURNAL

PAGE

	DATE		DESCRIPTION	POST. REF.	DEBIT	CREDIT	
1							1
2							2
3							3
4							4
5							5
6							6
7							7
8							8
9							9
10							10
11							11
12							12
13							13
14							14
15							15
16							16
17							17
18							18
19							19
20							20
21							21
22							22
23							23
24							24

EXERCISE 9-14, Concluded

Computations:

Aging Class (Number of Days Past Due)	Receivables Balance on Dec. 31	Estimated Doubtful Accounts Percent	Estimated Doubtful Accounts Amount
0–30 days	$300,000	1%	$ _____
31–60 days	80,000	4	_____
61–90 days	20,000	15	_____
91–120 days	10,000	40	_____
More than 120 days	40,000	80	_____
Total receivables	$450,000		_____
_____			$ _____
_____			_____
_____			_____

c.

_____

_____

EXERCISE 9-15

_____

_____

EXERCISE 9-16

a. _____

b. _____

EXERCISE 9-17

a.

		JOURNAL				PAGE	

	DATE		DESCRIPTION	POST. REF.	DEBIT	CREDIT	
1							1
2							2
3							3
4							4
5							5
6							6

b.

		JOURNAL				PAGE	

	DATE		DESCRIPTION	POST. REF.	DEBIT	CREDIT	
1							1
2							2
3							3
4							4
5							5
6							6
7							7
8							8
9							9
10							10

c. _____

_____

_____

_____

EXERCISE 9-18

a.

JOURNAL PAGE

	DATE		DESCRIPTION	POST. REF.	DEBIT	CREDIT	
1							1
2							2
3							3
4							4
5							5

b.

JOURNAL PAGE

	DATE		DESCRIPTION	POST. REF.	DEBIT	CREDIT	
1							1
2							2
3							3
4							4
5							5
6							6
7							7
8							8
9							9

c. _____

_____

_____

Computations:

Aging Class (Number of Days Past Due)	Receivables Balance on Dec. 31	Estimated Doubtful Accounts	
		Percent	Amount
0–30 days	$600,000	1%	$ _____
31–60 days	150,000	2	_____
61–90 days	75,000	18	_____
91–120 days	50,000	30	_____
More than 120 days	60,000	50	_____
Total receivables	$935,000		_____
			$ _____

EXERCISE 9-19

	Date of Note	Face Amount	Interest Rate	Term of Note	Due Date	Interest Due
a.	May 15	$ 40,000	6%	90 days	_____	$ _____
b.	March 20	15,000	4	60 days	_____	_____
c.	May 19	24,000	3	60 days	_____	_____
d.	October 1	10,500	8	60 days	_____	_____
e.	August 30	18,000	5	120 days	_____	_____

EXERCISE 9-20

a. _____

b. _____

c. (1) and (2)

JOURNAL   PAGE

	DATE		DESCRIPTION	POST. REF.	DEBIT	CREDIT	
1							1
2							2
3							3
4							4
5							5
6							6

EXERCISE 9-21

1. _____

2. _____

3. _____

4. _____

5. _____

6. _____

   _____

7. _____

   _____

EXERCISE 9-22

JOURNAL   PAGE

	DATE	DESCRIPTION	POST. REF.	DEBIT	CREDIT	
1						1
2						2
3						3
4						4
5						5
6						6
7						7
8						8
9						9
10						10
11						11
12						12
13						13
14						14
15						15
16						16
17						17
18						18

EXERCISE 9-23

JOURNAL   PAGE

	DATE	DESCRIPTION	POST. REF.	DEBIT	CREDIT	
1						1
2						2
3						3
4						4
5						5
6						6
7						7
8						8
9						9
10						10
11						11

EXERCISE 9-24

JOURNAL

	DATE		DESCRIPTION	POST. REF.	DEBIT	CREDIT	
1							1
2							2
3							3
4							4
5							5
6							6
7							7
8							8
9							9
10							10
11							11
12							12
13							13
14							14
15							15
16							16
17							17
18							18
19							19
20							20
21							21
22							22
23							23

EXERCISE 9-25

_____

_____

_____

_____

_____

_____

Optional

_____

Balance Sheet

_____

EXERCISE   9-26

a. and b.

	2009	**2008**
Net sales	_____	_____
Accounts receivable	_____	_____
Average accounts receivable	_____	_____
Accounts receivable turnover	_____	_____
Average daily sales	_____	_____
Days' sales in receivables	_____	_____

c. _____

_____

_____

_____

_____

_____

EXERCISE   9-27

a. and b.

	2009	**2008**
Net sales	_____	_____
Accounts receivable	_____	_____
Average accounts receivable	_____	_____
Accounts receivable turnover	_____	_____
Average daily sales	_____	_____
Days' sales in receivables	_____	_____

c. _____

_____

_____

_____

_____

EXERCISE   9-28

a. and b.

	For the Period Ending	
	Jan. 31, 2010	**Jan. 31, 2009**
Net sales	_____	_____
Accounts receivable	_____	_____
Average accounts receivable	_____	_____
Accounts receivable turnover	_____	_____
Average daily sales	_____	_____
Days' sales in receivables	_____	_____

c. _____

_____

_____

_____

_____

EXERCISE 9-29

a. The Limited Brands Inc.: _____

_____

H.J. Heinz Company: _____

_____

b. _____

c. _____

_____

_____

_____

_____

_____

_____

_____

_____

_____

_____

418

This Page Not Used.

PROBLEM 9-1 ___

1. and 2.

Allowance for Doubtful Accounts

Bad Debt Expense

3. _____

4. a. _____

   b. _____

   c. _____

PROBLEM   9-1 ___, Concluded

2.

JOURNAL   PAGE

	DATE	DESCRIPTION	POST. REF.	DEBIT	CREDIT	
1						1
2						2
3						3
4						4
5						5
6						6
7						7
8						8
9						9
10						10
11						11
12						12
13						13
14						14
15						15
16						16
17						17
18						18
19						19
20						20
21						21
22						22
23						23
24						24
25						25
26						26
27						27
28						28

PROBLEM   9-2 ___

1.

Customer	Due Date	Number of Days Past Due

4.

JOURNAL   PAGE _____

	DATE		DESCRIPTION	POST. REF.	DEBIT	CREDIT	
1							1
2							2
3							3
4							4
5							5
6							6
7							7

5. _____

_____

_____

_____

PROBLEM 9-2 ___, Concluded

2. and 3.

	A	B	C	D	E	F	G	H
	Customer	Balance	Not Past Due	1–30	31–60	61–90	Over 90	Over 120
1	Aging of Receivables Schedule							
2	December 31, 2011							
3				Days Past Due				
4	Customer	Balance	Not Past Due	1–30	31–60	61–90	Over 90	Over 120
5								
6								
30								
31								
32								
33								
34								
35								
36								
37								
38								
39								
40								
41								
42								

PROBLEM 9-3 ___

1.

Year	Bad Debt Expense			Balance of Allowance Account, End of Year
	Expense Actually Reported	Expense Based on Estimate	Increase (Decrease) in Amount of Expense	

2.

_____

_____

_____

_____

_____

_____

_____

_____

_____

_____

_____

_____

_____

_____

This Page Not Used.

PROBLEM 9-4 ___

1.

Note	(a) Due Date	(b) Interest Due at Maturity
1.		
2.		
3.		
4.		
5.		
6.		

2., 3., and 4.

JOURNAL

PAGE

	DATE		DESCRIPTION	POST. REF.	DEBIT	CREDIT	
1							1
2							2
3							3
4							4
5							5
6							6
7							7
8							8
9							9
10							10
11							11
12							12
13							13
14							14
15							15
16							16
17							17
18							18
19							19
20							20
21							21
22							22
23							23
24							24

426

This Page Not Used.

PROBLEM 9-5 ___

JOURNAL   PAGE

	DATE		DESCRIPTION	POST. REF.	DEBIT	CREDIT	
1							1
2							2
3							3
4							4
5							5
6							6
7							7
8							8
9							9
10							10
11							11
12							12
13							13
14							14
15							15
16							16
17							17
18							18
19							19
20							20
21							21
22							22
23							23
24							24
25							25
26							26
27							27
28							28
29							29
30							30
31							31
32							32
33							33
34							34
35							35
36							36

This Page Not Used.

PROBLEM 9-6 ___

JOURNAL   PAGE

	DATE		DESCRIPTION	POST. REF.	DEBIT	CREDIT	
1							1
2							2
3							3
4							4
5							5
6							6
7							7
8							8
9							9
10							10
11							11
12							12
13							13
14							14
15							15
16							16
17							17
18							18
19							19
20							20
21							21
22							22
23							23
24							24
25							25
26							26
27							27
28							28
29							29
30							30
31							31
32							32
33							33
34							34
35							35
36							36

PROBLEM 9-6 ___, Concluded

JOURNAL

PAGE

	DATE		DESCRIPTION	POST. REF.	DEBIT	CREDIT	
1							1
2							2
3							3
4							4
5							5
6							6
7							7
8							8
9							9
10							10
11							11
12							12
13							13
14							14
15							15
16							16
17							17
18							18
19							19
20							20
21							21
22							22
23							23
24							24
25							25
26							26
27							27
28							28
29							29
30							30
31							31
32							32
33							33
34							34
35							35
36							36

EXERCISE 10-1

a. New printing press costs debited to the asset account:

_____

_____

_____

_____

b. Used printing press costs debited to the asset account:

_____

_____

_____

_____

EXERCISE 10-2

a. _____

_____

_____

b. _____

_____

_____

EXERCISE 10-3

EXERCISE 10-4

1. _____
2. _____
3. _____
4. _____
5. _____
6. _____
7. _____
8. _____
9. _____
10. _____

EXERCISE 10-5

1. _____
2. _____
3. _____
4. _____
5. _____
6. _____
7. _____
8. _____
9. _____
10. _____

EXERCISE 10-6

JOURNAL

PAGE

	DATE	DESCRIPTION	POST. REF.	DEBIT	CREDIT	
1						1
2						2
3						3
4						4
5						5
6						6
7						7
8						8

EXERCISE 10-7

a. _____

_____

_____

_____

b. _____

_____

_____

_____

EXERCISE 10-8

a. 4 years: _____

b. 8 years: _____

c. 10 years: _____

d. 16 years: _____

e. 25 years: _____

f. 40 years: _____

g. 50 years: _____

EXERCISE 10-9

_____

_____

EXERCISE 10-10

_____

_____

_____

_____

EXERCISE 10-11

a.

Truck No.	Rate per Mile	Miles Operated	Credit to Accumulated Depreciation
1	_____	_____	$_____
2	_____	_____	$_____
3	_____	_____	$_____
4	_____	_____	$_____
Total			$_____

b.

JOURNAL   PAGE

	DATE		DESCRIPTION	POST. REF.	DEBIT	CREDIT	
1							1
2							2
3							3

EXERCISE 10-12

a. Straight-line method:

First year: _____

Second year: _____

b. Double-declining-balance method:

First year: _____

Second year: _____

EXERCISE 10-13

a. Straight-line method:

_____

b. Double-declining-balance method:

Year 1: _____

Year 2: _____

EXERCISE 10-14

a. Straight-line method:

Year 1: _____

Year 2: _____

b. Double-declining-balance method:

Year 1: _____

Year 2: _____

EXERCISE 10-15

a. _____

b. _____

c. _____

EXERCISE 10-16

a. and b.

JOURNAL   PAGE

	DATE		DESCRIPTION	POST. REF.	DEBIT	CREDIT	
1							1
2							2
3							3
4							4
5							5
6							6
7							7
8							8
9							9
10							10
11							11
12							12
13							13
14							14
15							15
16							16
17							17

EXERCISE 10-17

a.

b.(1) and (2)

JOURNAL   PAGE

	DATE		DESCRIPTION	POST. REF.	DEBIT	CREDIT	
1							1
2							2
3							3
4							4
5							5
6							6
7							7
8							8
9							9
17							17

EXERCISE 10-18

a. 2009: _____

2010: _____

2011: _____

b. _____

EXERCISE 10-18, Concluded

c. and d.

JOURNAL   PAGE

	DATE		DESCRIPTION	POST. REF.	DEBIT	CREDIT	
1							1
2							2
3							3
4							4
5							5
6							6
7							7
8							8
9							9
10							10
11							11
12							12
13							13
14							14
15							15
16							16
17							17

EXERCISE 10-19

a. _____

_____

b.

JOURNAL   PAGE

	DATE		DESCRIPTION	POST. REF.	DEBIT	CREDIT	
1							1
2							2
3							3
4							4

EXERCISE 10-20

a. _____

_____

b.

JOURNAL

	DATE		DESCRIPTION	POST. REF.	DEBIT	CREDIT	
1							1
2							2
3							3
4							4

EXERCISE 10-21

a.

	Current Year	Preceding Year	

_____

_____

_____

_____

_____

_____

EXERCISE 10-21, Concluded

b.

_____
_____
_____
_____
_____
_____
_____
_____

EXERCISE 10-22

_____
_____
_____
_____
_____
_____
_____
_____
_____
_____

EXERCISE 10-23

a. _____

_____

_____

b. _____

_____

_____

_____

_____

EXERCISE 10-24

a. _____

_____

b. _____

_____

_____

_____

_____

APPENDIX EXERCISE 10-25

a.

b.

APPENDIX EXERCISE 10-26

a.

b.

APPENDIX EXERCISE 10-27

a. and b.

JOURNAL

PAGE

	DATE		DESCRIPTION	POST. REF.	DEBIT	CREDIT	
1							1
2							2
3							3
4							4
5							5
6							6
7							7
8							8
9							9
10							10

APPENDIX   EXERCISE   10-28

a. and b.

JOURNAL

	DATE		DESCRIPTION	POST. REF.	DEBIT	CREDIT	
1							1
2							2
3							3
4							4
5							5
6							6
7							7
8							8
9							9
10							10

PROBLEM 10-1 ___

1. and 2.

Item	Land	Land Improvements	Building	Other Accounts
a.				
b.				
c.				
d.				
e.				
f.				
g.				
h.				
i.				
j.				
k.				
l.				
m.				
n.				
o.				
p.				
q.				
r.				
s.				
Total				

3.

_____

_____

_____

PROBLEM 10-1_, Concluded

4.

_____

_____

_____

_____

_____

_____

PROBLEM 10-2 ___

	Depreciation Expense		
Year	a. Straight-Line Method	b. Units-of-Production Method	c. Double-Declining-Balance Method
_____	_____	_____	_____
_____	_____	_____	_____
_____	_____	_____	_____
_____	_____	_____	_____
Total	================	================	================

Calculations:

_____

_____

_____

_____

_____

_____

_____

_____

_____

_____

_____

_____

_____

_____

_____

_____

_____

_____

_____

_____

_____

_____

PROBLEM 10-2_, Concluded

2.

_____

_____

_____

3.

_____

_____

_____

PROBLEM 10-3 ___

a.

Straight-Line Method

Year	Calculations	Depreciation Expense
2010		
2011		
2012		
2013		

b.

Units-of-Production Method

Year	Calculations	Depreciation Expense
2010		
2011		
2012		
2013		

c.

Double-Declining-Balance Method

Year	Calculations	Depreciation Expense
2010		
2011		
2012		
2013		

This Page Not Used.

PROBLEM 10-4 ___

1. a.

Straight-Line Method

Year	Depreciation Expense	Accumulated Depreciation, End of Year	Book Value, End of Year
1			
2			
3			
4			
5			

b.

Double-Declining-Balance Method

Year	Depreciation Expense	Accumulated Depreciation, End of Year	Book Value, End of Year
1			
2			
3			
4			
5			

PROBLEM 10-4 ___, Concluded

2.

JOURNAL PAGE

	DATE		DESCRIPTION	POST. REF.	DEBIT	CREDIT	
1							1
2							2
3							3
4							4
5							5
6							6
7							7
8							8
9							9
10							10
11							11
12							12
13							13
14							14

3.

JOURNAL PAGE

	DATE		DESCRIPTION	POST. REF.	DEBIT	CREDIT	
1							1
2							2
3							3
4							4
5							5
6							6
7							7
8							8
9							9
10							10
11							11
12							12
13							13
14							14

PROBLEM 10-5 ___

	DATE		DESCRIPTION	POST. REF.	DEBIT	CREDIT	
JOURNAL						PAGE	
1							1
2							2
3							3
4							4
5							5
6							6
7							7
8							8
9							9
10							10
11							11
12							12
13							13
14							14
15							15
16							16
17							17
18							18
19							19
20							20
21							21
22							22
23							23
24							24
25							25
26							26
27							27
28							28
29							29
30							30
31							31
32							32
33							33
34							34
35							35
36							36

PROBLEM 10-5 ___, Concluded

JOURNAL

	DATE	DESCRIPTION	POST. REF.	DEBIT	CREDIT	
1						1
2						2
3						3
4						4
5						5
6						6
7						7
8						8
9						9
10						10
11						11
12						12
13						13
14						14
15						15
16						16
17						17
18						18
19						19
20						20
21						21
22						22
23						23
24						24
25						25
26						26
27						27
28						28
29						29
30						30
31						31
32						32
33						33
34						34
35						35
36						36

PROBLEM 10-6 ___

1.

a. _____

_____

_____

b. _____

_____

_____

c. _____

_____

_____

2.

JOURNAL   PAGE

	DATE		DESCRIPTION	POST. REF.	DEBIT	CREDIT	
1							1
2							2
3							3
4							4
5							5
6							6
7							7
8							8
9							9
10							10
11							11
12							12

This Page Not Used.

EXERCISE 11-1

EXERCISE 11-2

a.(1) through b.(2)

JOURNAL

	DATE	DESCRIPTION	POST. REF.	DEBIT	CREDIT	
1						1
2						2
3						3
4						4
5						5
6						6
7						7
8						8
9						9
10						10
11						11
12						12
13						13
14						14
15						15
16						16
17						17
18						18
19						19
20						20

EXERCISE 11-3

a. _____

_____

b. (1) _____

(2) _____

c. _____

_____

_____

_____

_____

_____

_____

_____

_____

_____

_____

_____

EXERCISE 11-4

a. and b.

JOURNAL

PAGE

	DATE		DESCRIPTION	POST. REF.	DEBIT	CREDIT	
1							1
2							2
3							3
4							4
5							5
6							6
7							7
8							8
9							9
10							10
11							11
12							12
13							13
14							14

EXERCISE 11-5

a. and b.

	DATE		DESCRIPTION	POST. REF.	DEBIT	CREDIT	
1							1
2							2
3							3
4							4
5							5
6							6
7							7
8							8
9							9

JOURNAL PAGE

EXERCISE 11-6

a., b., and c.

JOURNAL PAGE

	DATE		DESCRIPTION	POST. REF.	DEBIT	CREDIT	
1							1
2							2
3							3
4							4
5							5
6							6
7							7
8							8
9							9
10							10
11							11
12							12

EXERCISE 11-7

a. _____

_____

b. _____

_____

c. _____

_____

EXERCISE 11-8

a.

b.

EXERCISE 11-9

	Consultant	Computer Programmer	Administrator
Regular earnings	$	$	$
Overtime earnings			
Gross pay	$	$	$
Less: Social security tax	$	$	$
Medicare tax			
Federal income tax withheld			
	$	$	$
Net pay	$	$	$

EXERCISE 11-9, Concluded

Withholding Supporting Calculations

	Consultant	Computer Programmer	Administrator

EXERCISE 11-10

a.

EXERCISE 11-10, Concluded

b. and c.

JOURNAL   PAGE

	DATE		DESCRIPTION	POST. REF.	DEBIT	CREDIT	
1							1
2							2
3							3
4							4
5							5
6							6
7							7
8							8
9							9
10							10
11							11
12							12
13							13
14							14
15							15
16							16

EXERCISE 11-11

a.

EXERCISE 11-11, Concluded

b.

			JOURNAL			PAGE	

	DATE		DESCRIPTION	POST. REF.	DEBIT	CREDIT	
1							1
2							2
3							3
4							4
5							5
6							6
7							7
8							8
9							9

EXERCISE 11-12

a.

			JOURNAL			PAGE	

	DATE		DESCRIPTION	POST. REF.	DEBIT	CREDIT	
1							1
2							2
3							3
4							4
5							5
6							6
7							7
8							8

b.

			JOURNAL			PAGE	

	DATE		DESCRIPTION	POST. REF.	DEBIT	CREDIT	
1							1
2							2
3							3
4							4
5							5
6							6
7							7
8							8

EXERCISE 11-13

a.

	DATE		DESCRIPTION	POST. REF.	DEBIT	CREDIT	
1							1
2							2
3							3
4							4
5							5
6							6
7							7
8							8
9							9

JOURNAL PAGE

b.

JOURNAL PAGE

	DATE		DESCRIPTION	POST. REF.	DEBIT	CREDIT	
1							1
2							2
3							3
4							4
5							5
6							6
7							7
8							8
9							9

EXERCISE 11-14

_____

_____

_____

_____

_____

_____

_____

_____

_____

EXERCISE 11-15

a. _____

_____

_____

_____

_____

b. _____

_____

_____

_____

_____

c. _____

_____

_____

_____

_____

d. _____

_____

_____

_____

_____

e. _____

_____

_____

_____

EXERCISE 11-16

a.

		JOURNAL				PAGE	
	DATE	DESCRIPTION	POST. REF.	DEBIT	CREDIT		
1							1
2							2
3							3
4							4

b. _____

_____

_____

_____

_____

_____

EXERCISE 11-17

a.

		JOURNAL				PAGE	
	DATE	DESCRIPTION	POST. REF.	DEBIT	CREDIT		
1							1
2							2
3							3
4							4
5							5
6							6

b. _____

_____

_____

_____

_____

_____

_____

_____

EXERCISE 11-18

_____
_____
_____
_____
_____
_____
_____
_____
_____
_____
_____
_____
_____
_____
_____
_____
_____

EXERCISE 11-19

a. and b.

JOURNAL

PAGE

	DATE		DESCRIPTION	POST. REF.	DEBIT	CREDIT	
1							1
2							2
3							3
4							4
5							5
6							6

EXERCISE 11-20

a.

_____

_____

_____

_____

_____

_____

b.

JOURNAL   PAGE

	DATE		DESCRIPTION	POST. REF.	DEBIT	CREDIT	
1							1
2							2
3							3
4							4

c.

_____

_____

_____

_____

_____

_____

EXERCISE 11-21

a.

JOURNAL   PAGE

	DATE		DESCRIPTION	POST. REF.	DEBIT	CREDIT	
1							1
2							2
3							3
4							4
5							5

EXERCISE 11-21, Concluded

b. _____

_____

_____

_____

_____

_____

_____

EXERCISE 11-22

a. December 31, 2011: _____

_____

December 31, 2012: _____

_____

b. _____

_____

_____

_____

_____

_____

_____

_____

_____

_____

_____

_____

_____

_____

_____

EXERCISE 11-23

a.

	Apple Computer, Inc:	Dell Inc.:
Quick Ratio:	_____	_____
Computations:		

_____

_____

_____

_____

_____

_____

_____

_____

_____

_____

b. _____

_____

_____

_____

_____

_____

_____

_____

_____

_____

_____

_____

_____

_____

_____

_____

This Page Not Used.

PROBLEM 11-1 ___

1.

JOURNAL   PAGE

	DATE		DESCRIPTION	POST. REF.	DEBIT	CREDIT	
1							1
2							2
3							3
4							4
5							5
6							6
7							7
8							8
9							9
10							10
11							11
12							12
13							13
14							14
15							15
16							16
17							17
18							18
19							19
20							20
21							21
22							22
23							23
24							24
25							25
26							26
27							27
28							28
29							29
30							30
31							31
32							32
33							33
34							34
35							35
36							36

PROBLEM 11-1 ___, Concluded

1. and 2.

JOURNAL

	DATE		DESCRIPTION	POST. REF.	DEBIT	CREDIT	
1							1
2							2
3							3
4							4
5							5
6							6
7							7
8							8
9							9
10							10
11							11
12							12
13							13
14							14
15							15
16							16
17							17
18							18
19							19
20							20
21							21
22							22
23							23
24							24
25							25
26							26
27							27
28							28
29							29
30							30
31							31
32							32
33							33
34							34
35							35
36							36

PROBLEM 11-2 ___

1.

			JOURNAL			PAGE		
	DATE		DESCRIPTION	POST. REF.	DEBIT	CREDIT		
1								1
2								2
3								3
4								4
5								5
6								6
7								7
8								8
9								9
10								10
11								11
12								12
13								13
14								14
15								15
16								16
17								17
18								18
19								19
20								20
21								21
22								22
23								23
24								24
25								25
26								26
27								27
28								28
29								29
30								30
31								31
32								32
33								33
34								34
35								35
36								36

PROBLEM 11-2 ___, Concluded

2.

JOURNAL

PAGE

	DATE		DESCRIPTION	POST. REF.	DEBIT	CREDIT	
1							1
2							2
3							3
4							4
5							5
6							6
7							7
8							8
9							9
10							10
11							11
12							12
13							13
14							14
15							15
16							16
17							17
18							18
19							19
20							20
21							21
22							22
23							23
24							24
25							25
26							26
27							27
28							28
29							29
30							30
31							31
32							32
33							33
34							34
35							35
36							36

PROBLEM 11-3 ___

1.

Employee	Gross Earnings	Federal Income Tax Withheld	Social Security Tax Withheld	Medicare Tax Withheld

_____

_____

_____

_____

_____

PROBLEM 11-3 ___, Concluded

2. Payroll taxes incurred and paid by employer:

   a. Social security tax paid by employer............................ $ _____

   b. Medicare tax paid by employer ....   _____

   c. State unemployment compensation tax.......................   _____

   Calculations and comments:

   _____

   _____

   _____

   _____

   _____

   _____

   d. Federal unemployment compensation tax ....   _____

   e. Total payroll tax expense .... $ _____

PROBLEM 11-4A

Knapp Company
PAYROLL FOR THE WEEK ENDED September 14, 2012

Name	Total Hrs	EARNINGS			DEDUCTION					PAID		ACCOUNTS DEBITED		
		Regular	Over-time	Total	SS Tax	Medi-care Tax	Federal Income Tax	Medical Insurance	Total	Net Pay	Ck. No.	Sales Salaries Expense	Office Salaries Expense	Delivery Salaries Expense
Baron, Red	42	800.00	60.00	860.00	51.60	12.90	137.60	65.00	267.10	592.90	801	860.00		
Brown, Charles	46	880.00	198.00	1,078.00	64.68	16.17	161.70	74.00	316.55	761.45	802	1,078.00		
Davis, Marci	40	840.00		840.00	50.40	12.60	121.80	59.00	243.80	596.20	803			840.00
Britton, Taylor		2,904.00		2,904.00	174.24	43.56	522.72	245.00	985.52	1,918.47	804		2,904.00	
Lewis, Lucy	45	1,040.00	195.00	1,235.00	74.10	18.53	216.13	96.00	404.75	830.25	805	1,235.00		
Mint, Patricia		1,982.00		1,982.00	118.92	29.73	356.76	115.00	620.41	1,361.59	806	1,982.00		
Newman, Alex	48	1,000.00	300.00	1,300.00	78.00	19.50	227.51	98.00	423.01	876.99	807		1,300.00	
Tracy, Rob	50	920.00	345.00	1,265.00	75.90	18.98	215.05	87.00	396.93	868.08	808			1,265.00
Van Pelt, Linus	38	735.00		735.00	44.108	11.03	102.90	78.00	236.03	498.98	809		735.00	
		11,101.00	1,098.00	12,199.00	731.94	182.99	2,062.17	917.00	3,894.09	8,304.90		5,155.00	4,204.00	2,840.00

PROBLEM 11-4B

Ritchie Manufacturing Company
PAYROLL FOR THE WEEK ENDED September 14, 2012

Name	Total Hours	EARNINGS			DEDUCTION					PAID		ACCOUNTS DEBITED		
		Regular	Over-time	Total	Social Secu-rity Tax	Medi-care Tax	Federal Income Tax	Medi-cal Insur-ance	Total	Net Pay	Ck. No.	Sales Salaries Expense	Office Salaries Expense	Delivery Salaries Expense
Buoy, JT	44	1,000.00	150.00	1,150.00	69.00	17.25	189.75	81.00	375.00	793.00	401	1,150.00		
Brown, Hope	43	1,120.00	126.00	1,246.00	74.76	18.69	186.90	87.00	367.35	878.65	402	1,246.00		
Chludzinski, Matt	40	1,406.00		1,406.00	84.36	21.09	210.90	98.00	414.35	991.65	403			1,406.00
Main, Aubrey		2,670.00		2,670.00	160.20	40.05	480.60	187.00	867.85	1,802.14	404		2,670.00	
McQuade, Hunter	47	1,208.00	294.00	1,502.00	90.12	22.53	277.87	105.00	495.52	1,006.48	405	1,50200		
Newman, Robert		2,500.00		2,500.00	150.00	37.50	460.90	175.00	823.40	1,676.60	406	2,500.00		
Setter, Lucy	46	1,200.00	270.00	1,470.00	88.20	22.05	257.25	103.00	470.50	999.50	407		1,470.00	
Warwick, Adam	52	1,120.00	504.00	1,624.00	97.44	24.36	243.60	114.00	479.39	1,144.61	408			1,624.00
Young, Doc	36	1,048.00		1,048.00	62.88	15.73	157.20	73.00	308.81	739.19	409			1,048.00
		13,272.00	1,344.00	14,616.00	876.96	219.25	2,464.97	1,023.00	3,908.28	9,803.72		6,398.00	4,140.00	4,078.00

PROBLEM 11-4 ___, Concluded

1. through 4.

JOURNAL

PAGE _____

	DATE		DESCRIPTION	POST. REF.	DEBIT	CREDIT	
1							1
2							2
3							3
4							4
5							5
6							6
7							7
8							8
9							9
10							10
11							11
12							12
13							13
14							14
15							15
16							16
17							17
18							18
19							19
20							20
21							21
22							22
23							23
24							24
25							25
26							26
27							27
28							28
29							29
30							30
31							31
32							32
33							33
34							34
35							35
36							36

This Page Not Used.

PROBLEM 11-5 ___

1. *The payroll register form is on pages 482-483.*

2.

JOURNAL   PAGE

	DATE		DESCRIPTION	POST. REF.	DEBIT	CREDIT	
1							1
2							2
3							3
4							4
5							5
6							6
7							7
8							8
9							9
10							10

PROBLEM 11-5 ___, Continued

1.

PAYROLL FOR WEEK ENDING

	NAME	TOTAL HOURS	EARNINGS			DEDUCTIONS		
			REGULAR	OVERTIME	TOTAL	SOCIAL SECURITY TAX	MEDICARE TAX	
1								1
2								2
3								3
4								4
5								5
6								6
7								7
8								8
9								9
10								10
11								11
12								12
13								13
14								14
15								15
16								16
17								17
18								18
19								19
20								20
21								21
22								22
23								23
24								24
25								25
26								26
27								27
28								28
29								29
30								30
31								31
32								32
33								33

PROBLEM 11-5 ___, Continued

December 7, 2012

	FEDERAL INCOME TAX	U.S. SAVINGS BONDS	TOTAL	PAID NET PAY	CK. NO.	ACCOUNTS DEBITED SALES SALARIES EXPENSE	OFFICE SALARIES EXPENSE	
1								1
2								2
3								3
4								4
5								5
6								6
7								7
8								8
9								9
10								10
11								11
12								12
13								13
14								14
15								15
16								16
17								17
18								18
19								19
20								20
21								21
22								22
23								23
24								24
25								25
26								26
27								27
28								28
29								29
30								30
31								31
32								32
33								33

PROBLEM 11-5 ___, Concluded

2.

JOURNAL

	DATE		DESCRIPTION	POST. REF.	DEBIT	CREDIT	
1							1
2							2
3							3
4							4
5							5
6							6
7							7
8							8
9							9
10							10

PROBLEM 11-6 ___

1.

		JOURNAL				PAGE

	DATE	DESCRIPTION	POST. REF.	DEBIT	CREDIT	
1						1
2						2
3						3
4						4
5						5
6						6
7						7
8						8
9						9
10						10
11						11
12						12
13						13
14						14
15						15
16						16
17						17
18						18
19						19
20						20
21						21
22						22
23						23
24						24
25						25
26						26
27						27
28						28
29						29
30						30
31						31
32						32
33						33
34						34
35						35
36						36

PROBLEM 11-6 ___, Continued

JOURNAL

PAGE _____

	DATE	DESCRIPTION	POST. REF.	DEBIT	CREDIT	
1						1
2						2
3						3
4						4
5						5
6						6
7						7
8						8
9						9
10						10
11						11
12						12
13						13
14						14
15						15
16						16
17						17
18						18
19						19
20						20
21						21
22						22
23						23
24						24
25						25
26						26
27						27
28						28
29						29
30						30
31						31
32						32
33						33
34						34
35						35
36						36

PROBLEM 11-6 ___ , Concluded

2.

JOURNAL   PAGE _____

	DATE		DESCRIPTION	POST. REF.	DEBIT	CREDIT	
1							1
2							2
3							3
4							4
5							5
6							6
7							7
8							8
9							9
10							10
11							11
12							12
13							13
14							14
15							15
16							16
17							17
18							18
19							19
20							20
21							21
22							22
23							23
24							24
25							25
26							26
27							27
28							28
29							29
30							30
31							31
32							32
33							33
34							34
35							35
36							36

488

This Page Not Used.

COMPREHENSIVE PROBLEM 3

1.

JOURNAL

	DATE		DESCRIPTION	POST. REF.	DEBIT	CREDIT	
1							1
2							2
3							3
4							4
5							5
6							6
7							7
8							8
9							9
10							10
11							11
12							12
13							13
14							14
15							15
16							16
17							17
18							18
19							19
20							20
21							21
22							22
23							23
24							24
25							25
26							26
27							27
28							28
29							29
30							30
31							31
32							32
33							33
34							34
35							35
36							36

COMPREHENSIVE PROBLEM 3, Continued

JOURNAL   PAGE ____

	DATE		DESCRIPTION	POST. REF.	DEBIT	CREDIT	
1							1
2							2
3							3
4							4
5							5
6							6
7							7
8							8
9							9
10							10
11							11
12							12
13							13
14							14
15							15
16							16
17							17
18							18
19							19
20							20
21							21
22							22
23							23
24							24
25							25
26							26
27							27
28							28
29							29
30							30
31							31
32							32
33							33
34							34
35							35
36							36

COMPREHENSIVE PROBLEM 3, Continued

2.

Bank Reconciliation		

COMPREHENSIVE PROBLEM 3, Continued

3. and 4.

JOURNAL

	DATE		DESCRIPTION	POST. REF.	DEBIT	CREDIT	
1							1
2							2
3							3
4							4
5							5
6							6
7							7
8							8
9							9
10							10
11							11
12							12
13							13
14							14
15							15
16							16
17							17
18							18
19							19
20							20
21							21
22							22
23							23
24							24
25							25
26							26
27							27
28							28
29							29
30							30
31							31
32							32
33							33
34							34
35							35
36							36

COMPREHENSIVE PROBLEM 3, Continued

JOURNAL

PAGE

	DATE	DESCRIPTION	POST. REF.	DEBIT	CREDIT	
1						1
2						2
3						3
4						4
5						5
6						6
7						7
8						8
9						9
10						10
11						11
12						12
13						13
14						14
15						15
16						16
17						17
18						18
19						19
20						20
21						21
22						22
23						23
24						24
25						25
26						26
27						27
28						28
29						29
30						30
31						31
32						32
33						33
34						34
35						35
36						36

Name

COMPREHENSIVE PROBLEM 3, Continued

5.

Balance Sheet

Name _____

COMPREHENSIVE PROBLEM 3, Continued

Chapter 11

COMPREHENSIVE PROBLEM 3, Concluded

6.

EXERCISE 12-1

JOURNAL

	DATE		DESCRIPTION	POST. REF.	DEBIT	CREDIT	
1							1
2							2
3							3
4							4
5							5
6							6
7							7

EXERCISE 12-2

JOURNAL

	DATE		DESCRIPTION	POST. REF.	DEBIT	CREDIT	
1							1
2							2
3							3
4							4
5							5
6							6
7							7
8							8
9							9

EXERCISE 12-3

		Wyatt	Truett
a.	....	_____	_____
b.	....	_____	_____
c.	....	_____	_____
d.	....	_____	_____
e.	....	_____	_____

Details

	Wyatt	Truett	Total
a.			
b.			
c.			
d.			
e.			

EXERCISE 12-4

	Wyatt	Truett
a.	_____	_____
b.	_____	_____
c.	_____	_____
d.	_____	_____
e.	_____	_____

Details

	Wyatt	Truett	Total
a.			
b.			
c.			
d.			
e.			

EXERCISE   12-5

	Ashley Adams	Michael Rovell	Total

EXERCISE   12-6

a.

_____

_____

_____

_____

_____

b.

_____

_____

_____

_____

_____

EXERCISE   12-7

a.

	Richards	Clark	Total

EXERCISE   12-7, Concluded

b. (1) and (2)

JOURNAL   PAGE _____

	DATE		DESCRIPTION	POST. REF.	DEBIT	CREDIT	
1							1
2							2
3							3
4							4
5							5
6							6
7							7
8							8
9							9
10							10
11							11

c. _____

_____

_____

_____

_____

_____

EXERCISE 12-8

a.

	WLKT Partners	Amanda Nelson	Daily Sentinel Newspaper, LLC	Total

b.

JOURNAL   PAGE

	DATE	DESCRIPTION	POST. REF.	DEBIT	CREDIT	
1						1
2						2
3						3
4						4
5						5
6						6
7						7
8						8
9						9
10						10
11						11
12						12

EXERCISE 12-8, Concluded

c.

	Statement of Members' Equity			
	WLKT Partners	Amanda Nelson	Daily Sentinel Newspaper, LLC	Total

d. _____

_____

_____

_____

_____

_____

_____

_____

EXERCISE   12-9

a., b., and c.

JOURNAL   PAGE

	DATE		DESCRIPTION	POST. REF.	DEBIT	CREDIT	
1							1
2							2
3							3
4							4
5							5
6							6
7							7
8							8
9							9
10							10
11							11
12							12

d. _____

_____

_____

_____

_____

_____

_____

EXERCISE   12-10

a. and b.

JOURNAL   PAGE

	DATE		DESCRIPTION	POST. REF.	DEBIT	CREDIT	
1							1
2							2
3							3
4							4
5							5
6							6

_____

_____

EXERCISE 12-11

a. (1) and (2)

JOURNAL   PAGE

	DATE		DESCRIPTION	POST. REF.	DEBIT	CREDIT	
1							1
2							2
3							3
4							4
5							5
6							6
7							7
8							8

b.

EXERCISE 12-12

a.

JOURNAL   PAGE

	DATE		DESCRIPTION	POST. REF.	DEBIT	CREDIT	
1							1
2							2
3							3
4							4
5							5
6							6
7							7
8							8

EXERCISE 12-12, Concluded

b.

c. _____

_____

_____

_____

_____

_____

_____

_____

EXERCISE   12-13

a.

EXERCISE 12-13, Concluded

b.

JOURNAL   PAGE

	DATE		DESCRIPTION	POST. REF.	DEBIT	CREDIT	
1							1
2							2
3							3
4							4
5							5
6							6

c. _____

_____

_____

_____

_____

_____

_____

_____

_____

EXERCISE 12-14

a.

JOURNAL

PAGE

	DATE		DESCRIPTION	POST. REF.	DEBIT	CREDIT	
1							1
2							2
3							3
4							4
5							5
6							6

b. (1)

JOURNAL

PAGE

	DATE		DESCRIPTION	POST. REF.	DEBIT	CREDIT	
1							1
2							2
3							3
4							4
5							5
6							6

Supporting calculations for the bonus:

EXERCISE   12-14, Concluded

b. (2)

JOURNAL   PAGE

	DATE	DESCRIPTION	POST. REF.	DEBIT	CREDIT	
1						1
2						2
3						3
4						4
5						5
6						6

Supporting calculations for the bonus:

EXERCISE   12-15

a.

JOURNAL   PAGE

	DATE	DESCRIPTION	POST. REF.	DEBIT	CREDIT	
1						1
2						2
3						3
4						4

EXERCISE   12-15, Concluded

b. (1)

JOURNAL

PAGE

	DATE		DESCRIPTION	POST. REF.	DEBIT	CREDIT	
1							1
2							2
3							3
4							4
5							5

Supporting calculations for the bonus:

b. (2)

JOURNAL

PAGE

	DATE		DESCRIPTION	POST. REF.	DEBIT	CREDIT	
1							1
2							2
3							3
4							4
5							5

Supporting calculations for the bonus:

EXERCISE 12-16

Statement of Partnership Equity

	Scott Wilson, Capital	Michael Goforth, Capital	Lance McGinnis, Capital	Total Partnership Capital	

<u>Calculations</u>

Admission of Lance McGinnis:

Net income distribution:

Withdrawals:

EXERCISE   12-17

a. and b.

JOURNAL   PAGE

	DATE		DESCRIPTION	POST. REF.	DEBIT	CREDIT	
1							1
2							2
3							3
4							4
5							5
6							6
7							7
8							8
9							9
10							10
11							11
12							12

EXERCISE   12-18

a. through f.

EXERCISE   12-18, Concluded

EXERCISE   12-19

a.

b. and c.

	Lyle	Fisher

EXERCISE 12-20

	Manson	Kumar	Total

EXERCISE 12-21

a. _____

b. _____

c.

JOURNAL

PAGE _____

	DATE		DESCRIPTION	POST. REF.	DEBIT	CREDIT	
1							1
2							2
3							3

Supporting calculations:

	Gifford	Lawrence	Ma

EXERCISE 12-22

a.

	Deacon	Raines	Francis	Total

b.

	Deacon	Raines	Francis	Total

EXERCISE 12-23

	Arnold	Peters	Suzuki

EXERCISE 12-24

Statement of Partnership Liquidation

	CASH	NONCASH ASSETS	LIABILITIES	CAPITAL		
				JESSUP	KING	OLIVER

EXERCISE 12-25

a.

Statement of LLC Liquidation

	CASH	NONCASH ASSETS	LIABILITIES	MEMBER EQUITY		
				HALL	LANG	DAS

b.

JOURNAL

PAGE

DATE	DESCRIPTION	POST. REF.	DEBIT	CREDIT	
					1
					2
					3
					4
					5

Name _____

Chapter 12

EXERCISE 12-25, Concluded

c.

EXERCISE 12-26

a. (1) and (2)

JOURNAL   PAGE ___

	DATE	DESCRIPTION	POST. REF.	DEBIT	CREDIT	
1						1
2						2
3						3
4						4
5						5
6						6
7						7
8						8
9						9
10						10
11						11
12						12

b.

Statement of Partners' Equity

	Gary Menendez	Melissa Breeden	Total

EXERCISE 12-27

a.

_____

_____

_____

_____

_____

_____

_____

_____

b.

_____

_____

_____

_____

_____

_____

_____

_____

_____

_____

EXERCISE 12-28

a.

_____

_____

_____

_____

_____

_____

_____

_____

b.

_____

_____

_____

_____

_____

_____

_____

_____

_____

_____

_____

_____

_____

PROBLEM 12-1___

1.

JOURNAL   PAGE

	DATE		DESCRIPTION	POST. REF.	DEBIT	CREDIT	
1							1
2							2
3							3
4							4
5							5
6							6
7							7
8							8
9							9
10							10
11							11
12							12

2.

Balance Sheet

PROBLEM 12-1___, Concluded

3.

JOURNAL

	DATE		DESCRIPTION	POST. REF.	DEBIT	CREDIT	
1							1
2							2
3							3
4							4
5							5
6							6
7							7
8							8
9							9
10							10
11							11
12							12
13							13
14							14
15							15
16							16
17							17
18							18

Computations:

PROBLEM 12-2___

	(1) Net Income of _____		(2) Net Income of _____	
Plan	Partner: _____	Partner: _____	Partner: _____	Partner: _____
a.				
b.				
c.				
d.				
e.				
f.				

Supporting calculations:

	Net Income of _____		Net Income of _____	

PROBLEM 12-2___, Concluded

	Net Income of _____		Net Income of _____	

PROBLEM 12-3___

1. _____

Income Statement

_____

Division of net income:

2. _____

Statement of Partners' Equity

_____

PROBLEM 12-3___, Concluded

3. _____

Balance Sheet

PROBLEM 12-4 ___

1. and 2.

JOURNAL

PAGE

	DATE	DESCRIPTION	POST. REF.	DEBIT	CREDIT	
1						1
2						2
3						3
4						4
5						5
6						6
7						7
8						8
9						9
10						10
11						11
12						12
13						13
14						14
15						15
16						16
17						17
18						18
19						19
20						20
21						21
22						22
23						23
24						24
25						25
26						26
27						27
28						28
29						29
30						30
31						31
32						32

PROBLEM 12-4___, Concluded

3.

PROBLEM 12-5 ___

1.

Statement of Partnership Liquidation

	CASH	NONCASH ASSETS	LIABILITIES	CAPITAL		

PROBLEM 12-5___, Concluded

2. a.

JOURNAL   PAGE

	DATE		DESCRIPTION	POST. REF.	DEBIT	CREDIT	
1							1
2							2
3							3
4							4

_____

_____

_____

_____

_____

_____

2. b.

JOURNAL   PAGE

	DATE		DESCRIPTION	POST. REF.	DEBIT	CREDIT	
1							1
2							2
3							3
4							4

PROBLEM 12-6

1. a.

Statement of Partnership Liquidation

	CASH	NONCASH ASSETS	LIABILITIES	CAPITAL		

PROBLEM 12-6___, Continued

1. b.

Statement of Partnership Liquidation

CASH	NONCASH ASSETS	LIABILITIES	CAPITAL		

PROBLEM 12-6___, Concluded

2. a.

	DATE		DESCRIPTION	POST. REF.	DEBIT	CREDIT	
1							1
2							2
3							3
4							4

JOURNAL — PAGE

_____
_____
_____
_____
_____
_____

2. b.

JOURNAL — PAGE

	DATE		DESCRIPTION	POST. REF.	DEBIT	CREDIT	
1							1
2							2
3							3
4							4

This Page Not Used.

EXERCISE 13-1

Description	1st Year	2nd Year	3rd Year	4th Year
Total dividend declared				
Preferred dividend (current)				
Preferred dividend in arrears				
Total preferred dividends				
Preferred shares outstanding				
Preferred dividend per share				
Dividend for common shares				
Common shares outstanding				
Common dividend per share				

EXERCISE 13-2

Description	1st Year	2nd Year	3rd Year	4th Year
Total dividend declared				
Preferred dividend (current)				
Preferred dividend in arrears				
Total preferred dividends				
Preferred shares outstanding				
Preferred dividend per share				
Dividend for common shares				
Common shares outstanding				
Common dividend per share				

EXERCISE 13-3

a.

	DATE		DESCRIPTION	POST. REF.	DEBIT	CREDIT	
1							1
2							2
3							3
4							4
5							5
6							6
7							7
8							8
9							9
10							10

JOURNAL — PAGE

b. _____

EXERCISE 13-4

a.

	DATE		DESCRIPTION	POST. REF.	DEBIT	CREDIT	
1							1
2							2
3							3
4							4
5							5
6							6
7							7
8							8
9							9
10							10

JOURNAL — PAGE

b. _____

EXERCISE 13-5

JOURNAL

	DATE	DESCRIPTION	POST. REF.	DEBIT	CREDIT	
1						1
2						2
3						3
4						4

EXERCISE 13-6

a., b., and c.

JOURNAL

PAGE

	DATE	DESCRIPTION	POST. REF.	DEBIT	CREDIT	
1						1
2						2
3						3
4						4
5						5
6						6
7						7
8						8
9						9
10						10
11						11
12						12
13						13
14						14
15						15

EXERCISE 13-7

JOURNAL

PAGE

	DATE	DESCRIPTION	POST. REF.	DEBIT	CREDIT	
1						1
2						2
3						3
4						4
5						5
6						6
7						7
8						8
9						9

EXERCISE 13-8

JOURNAL

PAGE

	DATE	DESCRIPTION	POST. REF.	DEBIT	CREDIT	
1						1
2						2
3						3
4						4
5						5
6						6
7						7
8						8
9						9
10						10
11						11
12						12
13						13
14						14
15						15
16						16
17						17
18						18

EXERCISE 13-9

JOURNAL   PAGE

	DATE		DESCRIPTION	POST. REF.	DEBIT	CREDIT	
1							1
2							2
3							3
4							4
5							5
6							6
7							7
8							8
9							9

EXERCISE 13-10

a. (1) and (2)

JOURNAL   PAGE

	DATE		DESCRIPTION	POST. REF.	DEBIT	CREDIT	
1							1
2							2
3							3
4							4
5							5
6							6
7							7
8							8
9							9

b. (1) Total paid-in capital: _____

   (2) Total retained earnings: _____

   (3) Total stockholders' equity: _____

c. (1) Total paid-in capital: _____

   (2) Total retained earnings: _____

   (3) Total stockholders' equity: _____

EXERCISE 13-11

a.

JOURNAL

	DATE		DESCRIPTION	POST. REF.	DEBIT	CREDIT	
1							1
2							2
3							3
4							4
5							5
6							6
7							7
8							8
9							9
10							10
11							11
12							12
13							13

b. _____

c. _____

_____

_____

_____

_____

_____

_____

EXERCISE 13-12

a.

JOURNAL PAGE

	DATE	DESCRIPTION	POST. REF.	DEBIT	CREDIT	
1						1
2						2
3						3
4						4
5						5
6						6
7						7
8						8
9						9
10						10
11						11
12						12
13						13
14						14
15						15

b. _____

c. _____

d. _____

_____

_____

_____

_____

_____

EXERCISE 13-13

a.

	DATE		DESCRIPTION	POST. REF.	DEBIT	CREDIT	
1							1
2							2
3							3
4							4
5							5
6							6
7							7
8							8
9							9
10							10
11							11
12							12
13							13
14							14
15							15
16							16
17							17
18							18
19							19

JOURNAL   PAGE

b. _____

c. _____

d. _____

_____

_____

_____

_____

_____

_____

_____

_____

EXERCISE 13-14

EXERCISE 13-15

EXERCISE 13-16

EXERCISE 13-17

Retained Earnings Statement

EXERCISE 13-18

_____

_____

_____

_____

_____

_____

_____

_____

_____

_____

_____

_____

_____

Corrected Stockholders' Equity section (optional):

Name _____

EXERCISE 13-19

Statement of Stockholders' Equity

EXERCISE 13-20

a. _____

b. _____

EXERCISE 13-21

	Assets	Liabilities	Stockholders' Equity
(1) Authorizing and issuing stock certificates in a stock split..	_____	_____	_____
(2) Declaring a stock dividend	_____	_____	_____
(3) Issuing stock certificates for the stock dividend declared in (2)......................................	_____	_____	_____
(4) Declaring a cash dividend...................................	_____	_____	_____
(5) Paying the cash dividend declared in (4).............	_____	_____	_____

EXERCISE 13-22

JOURNAL

PAGE _____

	DATE		DESCRIPTION	POST. REF.	DEBIT	CREDIT	
1							1
2							2
3							3
4							4
5							5
6							6
7							7
8							8
9							9
10							10
11							11
12							12
13							13
14							14
15							15
16							16
17							17
18							18
19							19
20							20
21							21
22							22
23							23
24							24
25							25
26							26
27							27
28							28

EXERCISE 13-23

EXERCISE 13-24

a.

b.

	2009	2008	2007	

EXERCISE 13-25

a. Office Max: _____

_____

_____

_____

_____

_____

Staples: _____

_____

_____

_____

_____

_____

b. _____

_____

_____

_____

_____

_____

_____

_____

PROBLEM 13-1 ___

1.

Year	Total Dividends	Preferred Dividends		Common Dividends	
		Total	Per Share	Total	Per Share
2007					
2008					
2009					
2010					
2011					
2012					

2.

Average annual dividend for preferred: _____

Average annual dividend for common: _____

3. a. _____

    b. _____

This Page Not Used.

PROBLEM 13-2 ___

	JOURNAL				PAGE

	DATE		DESCRIPTION	POST. REF.	DEBIT	CREDIT	
1							1
2							2
3							3
4							4
5							5
6							6
7							7
8							8
9							9
10							10
11							11
12							12
13							13
14							14
15							15
16							16
17							17
18							18
19							19
20							20
21							21
22							22
23							23
24							24
25							25
26							26
27							27
28							28
29							29
30							30
31							31
32							32
33							33
34							34
35							35
36							36

556

This Page Not Used.

PROBLEM 13-3 ___

a. through g.

JOURNAL

	DATE	DESCRIPTION	POST. REF.	DEBIT	CREDIT	
1						1
2						2
3						3
4						4
5						5
6						6
7						7
8						8
9						9
10						10
11						11
12						12
13						13
14						14
15						15
16						16
17						17
18						18
19						19
20						20
21						21
22						22
23						23
24						24
25						25
26						26
27						27
28						28
29						29
30						30
31						31
32						32
33						33
34						34
35						35
36						36

558

This Page Not Used.

PROBLEM 13-4 ___

1. and 2.

Common Stock

Paid-In Capital in Excess of Stated Value

Retained Earnings

Treasury Stock

Paid-In Capital from Sale of Treasury Stock

PROBLEM 13-4 ___, Continued

Stock Dividends Distributable

Stock Dividends

Cash Dividends

PROBLEM 13-4 ___, Continued

2.

JOURNAL

PAGE

	DATE		DESCRIPTION	POST. REF.	DEBIT	CREDIT	
1							1
2							2
3							3
4							4
5							5
6							6
7							7
8							8
9							9
10							10
11							11
12							12
13							13
14							14
15							15
16							16
17							17
18							18
19							19
20							20
21							21
22							22
23							23
24							24
25							25
26							26
27							27
28							28
29							29
30							30
31							31
32							32
33							33
34							34
35							35
36							36

PROBLEM 13-4 ___, Concluded

3.

Retained Earnings Statement		

4.

PROBLEM 13-5 ___

JOURNAL

PAGE

	DATE	DESCRIPTION	POST. REF.	DEBIT	CREDIT	
1						1
2						2
3						3
4						4
5						5
6						6
7						7
8						8
9						9
10						10
11						11
12						12
13						13
14						14
15						15
16						16
17						17
18						18
19						19
20						20
21						21
22						22
23						23
24						24
25						25
26						26
27						27
28						28
29						29
30						30
31						31
32						32
33						33
34						34
35						35
36						36

PROBLEM 13-5 ___, Concluded

JOURNAL

	DATE		DESCRIPTION	POST. REF.	DEBIT	CREDIT	
1							1
2							2
3							3
4							4
5							5
6							6
7							7
8							8
9							9
10							10
11							11
12							12
13							13
14							14
15							15
16							16
17							17
18							18
19							19
20							20
21							21
22							22
23							23
24							24
25							25
26							26
27							27
28							28
29							29
30							30
31							31
32							32
33							33
34							34
35							35
36							36

EXERCISE 14-1

	a.	b.	c.
Earnings before bond interest and income tax			
Bond interest			
Balance			
Income tax			
Net income			
Dividends on preferred stock			
Earnings available for common stock			
Earnings per share on common stock			

EXERCISE 14-2

_____

_____

_____

_____

_____

_____

_____

_____

_____

_____

_____

EXERCISE 14-3

_____

_____

_____

_____

_____

_____

_____

_____

_____

_____

EXERCISE 14-4

_____

_____

_____

_____

_____

_____

_____

_____

_____

_____

EXERCISE 14-5

JOURNAL

PAGE

	DATE		DESCRIPTION	POST. REF.	DEBIT	CREDIT	
1							1
2							2
3							3
4							4
5							5
6							6
7							7
8							8
9							9
10							10

EXERCISE 14-6

a. 1. through 4.

JOURNAL   PAGE

	DATE		DESCRIPTION	POST. REF.	DEBIT	CREDIT	
1							1
2							2
3							3
4							4
5							5
6							6
7							7
8							8
9							9
10							10
11							11
12							12
13							13

b.

c.

EXERCISE 14-7

a. and b.

JOURNAL

	DATE		DESCRIPTION	POST. REF.	DEBIT	CREDIT	
1							1
2							2
3							3
4							4
5							5
6							6
7							7
8							8
9							9
10							10

c.

_____

_____

_____

_____

_____

_____

_____

_____

EXERCISE 14-8

JOURNAL   PAGE

	DATE		DESCRIPTION	POST. REF.	DEBIT	CREDIT	
1							1
2							2
3							3
4							4
5							5
6							6
7							7
8							8
9							9
10							10
11							11
12							12
13							13

EXERCISE 14-9

JOURNAL   PAGE

	DATE		DESCRIPTION	POST. REF.	DEBIT	CREDIT	
1							1
2							2
3							3
4							4
5							5
6							6
7							7
8							8
9							9
10							10
11							11
12							12
13							13

EXERCISE 14-10

a. 1. and 2.

JOURNAL

PAGE

	DATE		DESCRIPTION	POST. REF.	DEBIT	CREDIT	
1							1
2							2
3							3
4							4
5							5
6							6
7							7
8							8
9							9
10							10

b. _____

_____

_____

_____

Current Liabilities:			
Noncurrent Liabilities:			

EXERCISE 14-11

JOURNAL   PAGE

	DATE	DESCRIPTION	POST. REF.	DEBIT	CREDIT	
1						1
2						2
3						3
4						4
5						5
6						6
7						7
8						8
9						9
10						10
11						11
12						12
13						13
14						14
15						15
16						16
17						17
18						18

EXERCISE 14-12

a.

	A	B	C	D	E
Amortization of Installment Notes					
For the Year Ending	**January 1 Carrying Amount**	**Note Payment (Cash Paid)**	**Interest Expense (9% of January 1 Note Carrying Amount)**	**Decrease in Notes Payable (B – C)**	**December 31 Carrying Amount (A – D)**

b.

JOURNAL   PAGE

	DATE		DESCRIPTION	POST. REF.	DEBIT	CREDIT	
1							1
2							2
3							3
4							4
5							5
6							6
7							7
8							8
9							9
10							10
11							11
12							12
13							13
14							14
15							15
16							16
17							17

EXERCISE 14-12, Concluded

JOURNAL   PAGE

	DATE		DESCRIPTION	POST. REF.	DEBIT	CREDIT	
1							1
2							2
3							3
4							4
5							5
6							6
7							7
8							8
9							9
10							10
11							11
12							12
13							13

c. _____

_____

EXERCISE 14-13

1. _____

_____

_____

_____

2. _____

_____

_____

_____

EXERCISE 14-14

a. _____

_____

_____

_____

_____

b. _____

EXERCISE 14-15

a. _____

_____

_____

_____

_____

b. _____

EXERCISE 14-16

a. _____

_____

_____

_____

_____

b. _____

APPENDIX 1 EXERCISE 14-17

_____

_____

_____

_____

_____

APPENDIX 1 EXERCISE 14-18

a.

b. _____

_____

c. _____

_____

APPENDIX 1 EXERCISE 14-19

_____

_____

_____

APPENDIX 1 EXERCISE 14-20

_____

_____

_____

APPENDIX 1 EXERCISE 14-21

APPENDIX 1 EXERCISE 14-22

APPENDIX 2 EXERCISE 14-23

a.

		JOURNAL			PAGE

	DATE	DESCRIPTION	POST. REF.	DEBIT	CREDIT	
1						1
2						2
3						3
4						4
5						5
6						6
7						7
8						8
9						9
10						10
11						11
12						12
13						13
14						14
15						15

b.

c.

APPENDIX 2 EXERCISE 14-24

a.

JOURNAL   PAGE

	DATE		DESCRIPTION	POST. REF.	DEBIT	CREDIT	
1							1
2							2
3							3
4							4
5							5
6							6
7							7
8							8
9							9
10							10
11							11
12							12
13							13
14							14
15							15

b.

c.

APPENDIX 2 EXERCISE 14-25

a. through d.

APPENDIX 2 EXERCISE 14-26

a. through d.

PROBLEM 14-1 ___

1.

	Plan 1	Plan 2	Plan 3
Earnings before interest and income tax			
Deduct interest on bonds			
Income before income tax			
Deduct income tax			
Net income			
Dividends on preferred stock			
Available for dividends on common stock			
Shares of common stock outstanding			
Earnings per share on common stock			

2.

	Plan 1	Plan 2	Plan 3
Earnings before interest and income tax			
Deduct interest on bonds			
Income before income tax			
Deduct income tax			
Net income			
Dividends on preferred stock			
Available for dividends on common stock			
Shares of common stock outstanding			
Earnings per share on common stock			

PROBLEM 14-1 ___ , Concluded

3.

_____

_____

_____

_____

_____

_____

_____

_____

_____

_____

_____

_____

_____

_____

_____

_____

_____

_____

_____

_____

_____

_____

_____

_____

_____

_____

_____

PROBLEM 14-2 ___

1. and 2.

JOURNAL PAGE

	DATE		DESCRIPTION	POST. REF.	DEBIT	CREDIT	
1							1
2							2
3							3
4							4
5							5
6							6
7							7
8							8
9							9
10							10
11							11
12							12
13							13
14							14
15							15
16							16
17							17
18							18
19							19
20							20
21							21
22							22
23							23
24							24
25							25

3.

PROBLEM 14-2 ___, Concluded

4.

_____

_____

_____

_____

_____

5.

PROBLEM 14-3 ___

1. and 2.

JOURNAL   PAGE

	DATE		DESCRIPTION	POST. REF.	DEBIT	CREDIT	
1							1
2							2
3							3
4							4
5							5
6							6
7							7
8							8
9							9
10							10
11							11
12							12
13							13
14							14
15							15
16							16
17							17
18							18
19							19
20							20
21							21
22							22
23							23
24							24
25							25

3.

_____

_____

PROBLEM 14-3 ___, Concluded

4.

_____

_____

_____

_____

_____

5.

PROBLEM 14-4 ___

1.

JOURNAL   PAGE

	DATE		DESCRIPTION	POST. REF.	DEBIT	CREDIT	
1							1
2							2
3							3
4							4
5							5
6							6
7							7
8							8
9							9
10							10
11							11
12							12
13							13
14							14
15							15
16							16
17							17
18							18
19							19
20							20
21							21
22							22
23							23
24							24
25							25
26							26
27							27
28							28
29							29
30							30
31							31
32							32
33							33
34							34
35							35
36							36

PROBLEM 14-4 ___, Concluded

JOURNAL   PAGE

	DATE	DESCRIPTION	POST. REF.	DEBIT	CREDIT	
1						1
2						2
3						3
4						4
5						5
6						6
7						7
8						8
9						9
10						10
11						11
12						12
13						13
14						14
15						15

2. (a) 2012: _____

   (b) 2013: _____

3.

APPENDIX 2 PROBLEM 14-5 ___

1. and 2.

JOURNAL PAGE

	DATE		DESCRIPTION	POST. REF.	DEBIT	CREDIT	
1							1
2							2
3							3
4							4
5							5
6							6
7							7
8							8
9							9
10							10
11							11
12							12
13							13
14							14
15							15
16							16
17							17
18							18
19							19

3.

_____

_____

_____

This Page Not Used.

APPENDIX 2 PROBLEM 14-6 ___

1. and 2.

	DATE		DESCRIPTION	POST. REF.	DEBIT	CREDIT	
1							1
2							2
3							3
4							4
5							5
6							6
7							7
8							8
9							9
10							10
11							11
12							12
13							13
14							14
15							15
16							16
17							17
18							18
19							19

JOURNAL   PAGE

3.

_____

_____

_____

_____

_____

_____

This Page Not Used.

EXERCISE 15-1

a. through d.

JOURNAL   PAGE

	DATE		DESCRIPTION	POST. REF.	DEBIT	CREDIT	
1							1
2							2
3							3
4							4
5							5
6							6
7							7
8							8
9							9
10							10
11							11
12							12
13							13
14							14
15							15
16							16
17							17
18							18
19							19
20							20
21							21
22							22

EXERCISE 15-2

a. through d.

<table>
<tr><th colspan="7" align="center">JOURNAL</th></tr>
<tr><th colspan="6"></th><th align="right">PAGE</th></tr>
<tr><th></th><th>DATE</th><th>DESCRIPTION</th><th>POST.
REF.</th><th>DEBIT</th><th>CREDIT</th><th></th></tr>
<tr><td>1</td><td></td><td></td><td></td><td></td><td></td><td>1</td></tr>
<tr><td>2</td><td></td><td></td><td></td><td></td><td></td><td>2</td></tr>
<tr><td>3</td><td></td><td></td><td></td><td></td><td></td><td>3</td></tr>
<tr><td>4</td><td></td><td></td><td></td><td></td><td></td><td>4</td></tr>
<tr><td>5</td><td></td><td></td><td></td><td></td><td></td><td>5</td></tr>
<tr><td>6</td><td></td><td></td><td></td><td></td><td></td><td>6</td></tr>
<tr><td>7</td><td></td><td></td><td></td><td></td><td></td><td>7</td></tr>
<tr><td>8</td><td></td><td></td><td></td><td></td><td></td><td>8</td></tr>
<tr><td>9</td><td></td><td></td><td></td><td></td><td></td><td>9</td></tr>
<tr><td>10</td><td></td><td></td><td></td><td></td><td></td><td>10</td></tr>
<tr><td>11</td><td></td><td></td><td></td><td></td><td></td><td>11</td></tr>
<tr><td>12</td><td></td><td></td><td></td><td></td><td></td><td>12</td></tr>
<tr><td>13</td><td></td><td></td><td></td><td></td><td></td><td>13</td></tr>
<tr><td>14</td><td></td><td></td><td></td><td></td><td></td><td>14</td></tr>
<tr><td>15</td><td></td><td></td><td></td><td></td><td></td><td>15</td></tr>
<tr><td>16</td><td></td><td></td><td></td><td></td><td></td><td>16</td></tr>
<tr><td>17</td><td></td><td></td><td></td><td></td><td></td><td>17</td></tr>
<tr><td>18</td><td></td><td></td><td></td><td></td><td></td><td>18</td></tr>
<tr><td>19</td><td></td><td></td><td></td><td></td><td></td><td>19</td></tr>
<tr><td>20</td><td></td><td></td><td></td><td></td><td></td><td>20</td></tr>
<tr><td>21</td><td></td><td></td><td></td><td></td><td></td><td>21</td></tr>
<tr><td>22</td><td></td><td></td><td></td><td></td><td></td><td>22</td></tr>
<tr><td>23</td><td></td><td></td><td></td><td></td><td></td><td>23</td></tr>
<tr><td>24</td><td></td><td></td><td></td><td></td><td></td><td>24</td></tr>
<tr><td>25</td><td></td><td></td><td></td><td></td><td></td><td>25</td></tr>
<tr><td>26</td><td></td><td></td><td></td><td></td><td></td><td>26</td></tr>
<tr><td>27</td><td></td><td></td><td></td><td></td><td></td><td>27</td></tr>
<tr><td>28</td><td></td><td></td><td></td><td></td><td></td><td>28</td></tr>
<tr><td>29</td><td></td><td></td><td></td><td></td><td></td><td>29</td></tr>
<tr><td>30</td><td></td><td></td><td></td><td></td><td></td><td>30</td></tr>
<tr><td>31</td><td></td><td></td><td></td><td></td><td></td><td>31</td></tr>
<tr><td>32</td><td></td><td></td><td></td><td></td><td></td><td>32</td></tr>
<tr><td>33</td><td></td><td></td><td></td><td></td><td></td><td>33</td></tr>
<tr><td>34</td><td></td><td></td><td></td><td></td><td></td><td>34</td></tr>
<tr><td>35</td><td></td><td></td><td></td><td></td><td></td><td>35</td></tr>
<tr><td>36</td><td></td><td></td><td></td><td></td><td></td><td>36</td></tr>
</table>

EXERCISE 15-3

a. through d.

| | | | | | | JOURNAL | | | | | PAGE | |

<table>
<tr><th colspan="2">DATE</th><th>DESCRIPTION</th><th>POST. REF.</th><th>DEBIT</th><th>CREDIT</th><th></th></tr>
<tr><td></td><td></td><td></td><td></td><td></td><td></td><td>1</td></tr>
<tr><td></td><td></td><td></td><td></td><td></td><td></td><td>2</td></tr>
<tr><td></td><td></td><td></td><td></td><td></td><td></td><td>3</td></tr>
<tr><td></td><td></td><td></td><td></td><td></td><td></td><td>4</td></tr>
<tr><td></td><td></td><td></td><td></td><td></td><td></td><td>5</td></tr>
<tr><td></td><td></td><td></td><td></td><td></td><td></td><td>6</td></tr>
<tr><td></td><td></td><td></td><td></td><td></td><td></td><td>7</td></tr>
<tr><td></td><td></td><td></td><td></td><td></td><td></td><td>8</td></tr>
<tr><td></td><td></td><td></td><td></td><td></td><td></td><td>9</td></tr>
<tr><td></td><td></td><td></td><td></td><td></td><td></td><td>10</td></tr>
</table>

EXERCISE 15-4

a. and b.

JOURNAL   PAGE _____

	DATE		DESCRIPTION	POST. REF.	DEBIT	CREDIT	
1							1
2							2
3							3
4							4
5							5
6							6
7							7
8							8
9							9
10							10
11							11
12							12
13							13
14							14
15							15
16							16
17							17
18							18
19							19
20							20
21							21
22							22
23							23
24							24
25							25

EXERCISE 15-5

EXERCISE 15-6

a., b., and c.

JOURNAL   PAGE

	DATE	DESCRIPTION	POST. REF.	DEBIT	CREDIT	
1						1
2						2
3						3
4						4
5						5
6						6
7						7
8						8
9						9
10						10
11						11
12						12
13						13
14						14
15						15

EXERCISE 15-7

JOURNAL   PAGE

	DATE	DESCRIPTION	POST. REF.	DEBIT	CREDIT	
1						1
2						2
3						3
4						4
5						5
6						6
7						7
8						8
9						9
10						10
11						11
12						12
13						13
14						14
15						15

EXERCISE 15-8

JOURNAL

PAGE

	DATE		DESCRIPTION	POST. REF.	DEBIT	CREDIT	
1							1
2							2
3							3
4							4
5							5
6							6
7							7
8							8
9							9
10							10
11							11
12							12
13							13
14							14
15							15
16							16
17							17
18							18
19							19
20							20
21							21
22							22
23							23
24							24

EXERCISE 15-9

JOURNAL

	DATE	DESCRIPTION	POST. REF.	DEBIT	CREDIT	
1						1
2						2
3						3
4						4
5						5
6						6
7						7
8						8
9						9
10						10
11						11
12						12
13						13
14						14
15						15
16						16
17						17
18						18
19						19
20						20
21						21
22						22
23						23
24						24

EXERCISE 15-10

a. and b.

JOURNAL   PAGE _____

	DATE		DESCRIPTION	POST. REF.	DEBIT	CREDIT	
1							1
2							2
3							3
4							4
5							5
6							6
7							7
8							8
9							9

c.

_____

_____

_____

_____

EXERCISE 15-11

a.

JOURNAL   PAGE _____

	DATE		DESCRIPTION	POST. REF.	DEBIT	CREDIT	
1							1
2							2
3							3
4							4
5							5
6							6
7							7
8							8
9							9
10							10
11							11
12							12
13							13
14							14

EXERCISE 15-11, Concluded

b.

EXERCISE 15-12

a.   **JOURNAL**   PAGE

	DATE	DESCRIPTION	POST. REF.	DEBIT	CREDIT	
1						1
2						2
3						3
4						4
5						5
6						6
7						7
8						8
9						9
10						10
11						11
12						12
13						13
14						14

b.

EXERCISE 15-12, Concluded

c. _____

_____

_____

_____

_____

_____

_____

_____

EXERCISE 15-13

EXERCISE 15-14

KVS Capital, Inc.

Selected Income Statement Items

For the Years Ended December 31, 2012 and 2013

	2012	2013
Operating income	a. _____	e. _____
Unrealized gain (loss)	b. _____	$ (3,000)
Net income	c. _____	19,000

Lydell Capital, Inc.

Selected Balance Sheet Items

December 31, 2011, 2012, and 2013

	Dec. 31, 2011	Dec. 31, 2012	Dec. 31, 2013
Trading investments, at cost	$123,000	$146,000	$172,000
Valuation allowance for investments	(4,000)	9,000	g. _____
Trading investments, at fair value	d. _____	f. _____	h. _____
Retained earnings	$156,000	$192,000	i. _____

EXERCISE 15-15

a.

JOURNAL   PAGE _____

	DATE		DESCRIPTION	POST. REF.	DEBIT	CREDIT	
1							1
2							2
3							3
4							4
5							5
6							6
7							7
8							8
9							9
10							10
11							11
12							12
13							13
14							14
15							15
16							16

b. _____

_____

_____

_____

_____

_____

EXERCISE 15-16

a. and b.

JOURNAL   PAGE

	DATE		DESCRIPTION	POST. REF.	DEBIT	CREDIT	
1							1
2							2
3							3
4							4
5							5
6							6
7							7
8							8
9							9
10							10
11							11
12							12
13							13
14							14
15							15
16							16
17							17
18							18
19							19
20							20

EXERCISE 15-17

a.

JOURNAL   PAGE

	DATE		DESCRIPTION	POST. REF.	DEBIT	CREDIT	
1							1
2							2
3							3
4							4
5							5
6							6
7							7

Computations:

b. _____

_____

_____

_____

_____

EXERCISE 15-18

a.

b.

EXERCISE 15-19

Oceanic Airways

Selected Income Statement Items

For the Years Ended December 31, 2012 and 2013

	2010	2011
Operating income	a. _____	g. _____
Gain (loss) from sale of investments	$4,000	$ (8,000)
Net income	b. _____	(15,000)

Oceanic Airways

Selected Balance Sheet Items

December 31, 2011, 2012, and 2013

	Dec. 31, 2009	Dec. 31, 2010	Dec. 31, 2011
Assets			
Available-for-sale investments, at cost	$ 78,000	$ 68,000	$95,000
Valuation allowance for available-for-sale investments	6,000	(9,000)	h. _____
Available-for-sale investments, at fair value	c. _____	e. _____	i. _____
Stockholders' Equity			
Unrealized gain (loss) on available-for-sale investments	d. _____	f. _____	(11,000)
Retained earnings	$151,000	$201,000	j. _____

EXERCISE 15-20

a.

	DATE		DESCRIPTION	POST. REF.	DEBIT	CREDIT	
1							1
2							2
3							3
4							4
5							5
6							6
7							7
8							8
9							9
10							10
11							11
12							12
13							13
14							14
15							15
16							16
17							17
18							18
19							19
20							20

JOURNAL   PAGE

b. _____

_____

_____

_____

_____

_____

_____

EXERCISE 15-21

a.

		JOURNAL				PAGE

	DATE		DESCRIPTION	POST. REF.	DEBIT	CREDIT	
1							1
2							2
3							3
4							4
5							5
6							6
7							7
8							8
9							9
10							10
11							11
12							12
13							13
14							14
15							15

b. _____

_____

_____

_____

_____

_____

_____

_____

EXERCISE 15-22

a.

		JOURNAL				PAGE

	DATE		DESCRIPTION	POST. REF.	DEBIT	CREDIT	
1							1
2							2
3							3
4							4
5							5
6							6
7							7

EXERCISE 15-22, Concluded

Computations:

b. _____

_____

_____

_____

_____

_____

_____

_____

EXERCISE 15-23

a.

_____

Balance Sheet (selected items)

EXERCISE 15-23, Concluded

b.

	Balance Sheet (selected items)		

EXERCISE 15-24

	Stockholders' Equity	

APPENDIX EXERCISE 15-25

Statement of Comprehensive Income		

APPENDIX EXERCISE 15-26

Statement of Comprehensive Income		

EXERCISE 15-27

Dividend Yield: _____

_____

_____

_____

_____

EXERCISE 15-28

a. 2008: Dividend Yield: _____

   2009: Dividend Yield: _____

b. _____

_____

_____

_____

_____

_____

_____

_____

_____

_____

EXERCISE 15-29

_____

_____

_____

_____

_____

_____

_____

_____

This Page Not Used.

PROBLEM 15-1 ___

1.

JOURNAL   PAGE

	DATE		DESCRIPTION	POST. REF.	DEBIT	CREDIT	
1	2012						1
2							2
3							3
4							4
5							5
6							6
7							7
8							8
9							9
10							10
11							11
12							12
13							13
14							14
15							15
16							16
17							17
18							18
19							19
20							20
21							21
22							22
23							23
24							24
25							25
26							26
27							27
28							28
29							29
30							30
31							31
32							32
33							33
34							34
35							35
36							36

PROBLEM 15-1 ___, Concluded

2.

_____

_____

_____

_____

_____

_____

_____

PROBLEM 15-2 ___

1.   **JOURNAL**   PAGE

	DATE		DESCRIPTION	POST. REF.	DEBIT	CREDIT	
1	2012						1
2							2
3							3
4							4
5							5
6							6
7							7
8							8
9							9
10							10
11							11
12							12
13							13
14							14
15							15
16							16
17							17
18							18
19							19
20							20
21							21
22							22
23							23

Calculations:

PROBLEM 15-2 ___, Continued

1.   **JOURNAL**   PAGE

	DATE		DESCRIPTION	POST. REF.	DEBIT	CREDIT	
1	2013						1
2							2
3							3
4							4
5							5
6							6
7							7
8							8
9							9
10							10
11							11
12							12
13							13
14							14
15							15
16							16
17							17
18							18
19							19

PROBLEM 15-2 ___, Concluded

2.

Balance Sheet (selected items)		

3. _____

_____

_____

_____

_____

_____

_____

_____

_____

This Page Not Used.

PROBLEM 15-3 ___

1.

JOURNAL   PAGE

	DATE		DESCRIPTION	POST. REF.	DEBIT	CREDIT	
1	2012						1
2							2
3							3
4							4
5							5
6							6
7							7
8							8
9							9
10							10
11							11
12							12
13							13
14							14
15							15
16							16
17							17
18							18
19							19
20							20
21							21
22							22
23							23
24							24
25							25
26							26
27							27
28							28
29							29
30							30
31							31
32							32
33							33
34							34
35							35
36							36

PROBLEM 15-3 ___, Continued

JOURNAL

	DATE		DESCRIPTION	POST. REF.	DEBIT	CREDIT	
1	2013						1
2							2
3							3
4							4
5							5
6							6
7							7
8							8
9							9
10							10
11							11
12							12
13							13
14							14
15							15
16							16
17							17
18							18
19							19
20							20
21							21
22							22
23							23
24							24

PROBLEM 15-3 ___, Concluded

2.

	Balance Sheet (selected items)		

624

This Page Not Used.

PROBLEM 15-4 ___

1. a. _____

    b. _____

    c. _____

Calculations:

    d. _____

    e. _____

    f. _____

    g. _____

    h. _____

    i. _____

PROBLEM 15-4 ___, Continued

Completed comparative unclassified balance sheet (optional):

		Balance Sheet		DEC. 31, 2013	DEC. 31, 2012

For December 31, 2013:

PROBLEM 15-4 ___, Concluded

For December 31, 2013:

628

This Page Not Used.

COMPREHENSIVE PROBLEM 4

1.

JOURNAL   PAGE

	DATE		DESCRIPTION	POST. REF.	DEBIT	CREDIT	
1							1
2							2
3							3
4							4
5							5
6							6
7							7
8							8
9							9
10							10
11							11
12							12
13							13
14							14
15							15
16							16
17							17
18							18
19							19
20							20
21							21
22							22
23							23
24							24
25							25
26							26
27							27
28							28
29							29
30							30
31							31
32							32
33							33
34							34
35							35
36							36

COMPREHENSIVE PROBLEM 4, Continued

JOURNAL

	DATE		DESCRIPTION	POST. REF.	DEBIT	CREDIT	
1							1
2							2
3							3
4							4
5							5
6							6
7							7
8							8
9							9
10							10
11							11
12							12
13							13
14							14
15							15
16							16
17							17
18							18
19							19
20							20
21							21
22							22
23							23
24							24
25							25
26							26
27							27
28							28
29							29
30							30
31							31
32							32
33							33
34							34
35							35
36							36

COMPREHENSIVE PROBLEM 4, Continued

JOURNAL

PAGE

	DATE	DESCRIPTION	POST. REF.	DEBIT	CREDIT	
1						1
2						2
3						3
4						4
5						5
6						6
7						7
8						8
9						9
10						10
11						11
12						12
13						13
14						14
15						15
16						16
17						17
18						18
19						19
20						20
21						21
22						22
23						23
24						24
25						25
26						26
27						27
28						28
29						29
30						30
31						31
32						32
33						33
34						34
35						35
36						36

COMPREHENSIVE PROBLEM 4, Continued

2. a.

Income Statement			

COMPREHENSIVE PROBLEM 4, Continued

b.

	Retained Earnings Statement			

COMPREHENSIVE PROBLEM 4, Continued

c.

Balance Sheet			

COMPREHENSIVE PROBLEM 4, Concluded

Balance Sheet (continued)

This Page Not Used.

EXERCISE 16-1

_____

_____

_____

_____

_____

_____

_____

_____

_____

_____

EXERCISE 16-2

a. _____

b. _____

c. _____

d. _____

e. _____

f. _____

g. _____

h. _____

EXERCISE 16-3

a. Sold equipment: _____

b. Issued bonds: _____

c. Issued common stock: _____

d. Paid cash dividends: _____

e. Purchased treasury stock: _____

f. Redeemed bonds: _____

g. Purchased patents: _____

h. Purchased buildings: _____

i. Sold long-term investments: _____

j. Issued preferred stock: _____

k. Net income: _____

EXERCISE 16-4

a. Decrease in accounts payable: _____

b. Increase in notes receivable due in 90 days from customers: _____

c. Decrease in accounts receivable: _____

d. Loss on disposal of fixed assets: _____

e. Increase in notes payable due in 90 days to vendors: _____

f. Amortization of patent: _____

g. Depreciation of fixed assets: _____

h. Gain on retirement of long-term debt: _____

i. Decrease in salaries payable: _____

j. Increase in merchandise receivable: _____

k. Decrease in prepaid expenses: _____

EXERCISE 16-5

a.

EXERCISE 16-5, Concluded

b. _____

_____

_____

_____

_____

_____

_____

_____

_____

_____

EXERCISE 16-6

a.

b. _____

_____

_____

_____

EXERCISE 16-7

a.

EXERCISE 16-7, Concluded

b. _____
_____
_____
_____
_____
_____
_____
_____
_____
_____

EXERCISE 16-8

_____
_____
_____
_____
_____
_____
_____
_____
_____
_____

EXERCISE 16-9

_____
_____
_____
_____
_____
_____
_____
_____
_____
_____

EXERCISE 16-10

_____
_____
_____
_____
_____
_____
_____
_____
_____

EXERCISE 16-11

_____
_____
_____
_____
_____
_____
_____
_____
_____
_____
_____
_____

EXERCISE 16-12

_____
_____
_____
_____
_____
_____
_____
_____
_____
_____
_____

EXERCISE 16-13

_____
_____
_____
_____
_____
_____
_____
_____
_____

EXERCISE 16-14

_____
_____
_____
_____
_____
_____
_____
_____

EXERCISE 16-15

a.

b.

_____

_____

_____

_____

_____

_____

_____

_____

_____

_____

_____

_____

_____

EXERCISE 16-16

a.

Cash Flows from Operating Activities		

b.

EXERCISE 16-17

a.

Statement of Cash Flows		

EXERCISE 16-17, Concluded

b.

EXERCISE 16-18

EXERCISE 16-18, Concluded
(Optional)

Statement of Cash Flows

EXERCISE 16-19

a. _____

_____

_____

_____

_____

_____

b. _____

_____

_____

_____

_____

_____

c. _____

_____

_____

_____

EXERCISE 16-20

EXERCISE 16-21

a.

b.

EXERCISE 16-22

a.

Computations:

b.

EXERCISE 16-23

Computations:

EXERCISE 16-24

a.

b.

_____

_____

_____

_____

_____

EXERCISE 16-25

a.

	FISCAL YEAR ENDED MAY 31, 2010 (all numbers in thousands)

EXERCISE 16-25, Concluded

b. _____

_____

_____

_____

_____

c. _____

_____

_____

_____

_____

_____

EXERCISE 16-26

_____

_____

_____

_____

_____

_____

_____

This Page Not Used.

PROBLEM 16-1 ___

Statement of Cash Flows

PROBLEM 16-1 ___, Concluded

The use of this form is not required unless so indicated by the instructor.

	A	B	C	D	E
1					
2		Spreadsheet (Work Sheet) for Statement of Cash Flows			
3					
4					
5		Balance,	Transactions		Balance,
6			Debit	Credit	
7					
8					
9					
10					
11					
12					
13					
14					
15					
16					
17					
18					
19					
20					
21					
22					
23					
24					
25					
26					
27					
28					
29					
30					
31					
32					
33					
34					
35					
36					
37					

PROBLEM 16-2 ___

Statement of Cash Flows			

PROBLEM 16-2 ___, Continued

The use of this form is not required unless so indicated by the instructor.

	A	B	C	D	E
1					
2		Spreadsheet (Work Sheet) for Statement of Cash Flows			
3					
4					
5		Balance,	Transactions		Balance,
6			Debit	Credit	
7					
8					
9					
10					
11					
12					
13					
14					
15					
16					
17					
18					
19					
20					
21					
22					
23					
24					
25					
26					
27					
28					
29					
30					
31					
32					

PROBLEM 16-2 ___, Concluded

The use of this form is not required unless so indicated by the instructor.

	A	B	C	D	E
1					
2		**Spreadsheet (Work Sheet) for Statement of Cash Flows**			
3					
4					
5		**Balance,**	**Transactions**		**Balance,**
6		_____	**Debit**	**Credit**	_____
7					
8					
9					
10					
11					
12					
13					
14					
15					
16					
17					
18					
19					
20					
21					
22					
23					
24					
25					

This Page Not Used.

PROBLEM 16-3 ___

Statement of Cash Flows				

PROBLEM 16-3 ___, Concluded

The use of this form is not required unless so indicated by the instructor.

	A	B	C	D	E
1					
2		**Spreadsheet (Work Sheet) for Statement of Cash Flows**			
3					
4					
5		**Balance,**	**Transactions**		**Balance,**
6		**_____**	**Debit**	**Credit**	**_____**
7					
8					
9					
10					
11					
12					
13					
14					
15					
16					
17					
18					
19					
20					
21					
22					
23					
24					
25					
26					
27					
28					
29					
30					
31					
32					
33					
34					
35					
36					
37					
38					
39					
40					
41					

PROBLEM 16-4 ___

Statement of Cash Flows

PROBLEM 16-4 ___, Concluded

	Statement of Cash Flows (continued)		

Computations:

PROBLEM 16-5 ___

Statement of Cash Flows

PROBLEM 16-5 ___, Concluded

Statement of Cash Flows (continued)			

Computations:

EXERCISE 17-1

a.

	2012		2011	
	AMOUNT	PERCENT	AMOUNT	PERCENT

Comparative Income Statement

b. _____

_____

_____

_____

_____

_____

_____

EXERCISE 17-2

a.

Comparative Income Statement (in thousands of dollars)

	2008		2007	
	AMOUNT	PERCENT	AMOUNT	PERCENT

b. _____

_____

_____

_____

_____

_____

_____

_____

_____

_____

_____

_____

_____

_____

EXERCISE 17-3

a.

	Common-Sized Income Statement			

	SHOESMITH ELECTRONICS COMPANY		ELECTRONICS INDUSTRY AVERAGE
	AMOUNT	PERCENT	

b. _____

_____

_____

_____

_____

_____

_____

_____

_____

_____

_____

_____

EXERCISE 17-4

Comparative Balance Sheet

	2012		2011	
	AMOUNT	PERCENT	AMOUNT	PERCENT

EXERCISE 17-5

a.

Comparative Income Statement

	2012 AMOUNT	2011 AMOUNT	INCREASE (DECREASE)	
			AMOUNT	PERCENT

b. _____

_____

_____

_____

_____

_____

_____

_____

EXERCISE 17-6

a. (1) Working Capital = _____

_____

2012: _____

_____

2011: _____

_____

(2) Current Ratio = _____

_____

2012: _____

_____

2011: _____

_____

(3) Quick Ratio = _____

_____

2012: _____

_____

2011: _____

_____

b. _____

_____

_____

_____

_____

_____

EXERCISE 17-7

a. (1) Current Ratio = _____

_____

Dec. 26, 2009: _____

_____

Dec. 27, 2008: _____

_____

EXERCISE 17-7, Concluded

(2) Quick Ratio = _____

_____

Dec. 26, 2009: _____

_____

Dec. 27, 2008: _____

_____

b. _____

_____

_____

_____

_____

_____

_____

_____

_____

EXERCISE 17-8

a. _____

_____

_____

_____

_____

_____

_____

_____

_____

_____

_____

_____

The correct calculations are:

Working Capital = _____

_____

Current Ratio = _____

_____

Quick Ratio = _____

_____

EXERCISE 17-8, Concluded

b. _____
_____
_____
_____
_____
_____

EXERCISE 17-9

a. (1) Accounts Receivable Turnover = _____
_____

    2012: _____
_____

    2011: _____
_____

  (2) Number of Days' Sales in Receivables = _____
_____

    2012: _____
_____

    2011: _____
_____
_____
_____
_____

b. _____
_____
_____
_____
_____
_____
_____
_____
_____
_____

EXERCISE 17-10

a. (1) Accounts Receivable Turnover = _____

_____

Klick: _____

_____

Klack: _____

_____

(2) Number of Days' Sales in Receivables = _____

_____

Klick: _____

_____

Klack: _____

_____

_____

_____

b. _____

_____

_____

_____

_____

_____

_____

_____

_____

EXERCISE 17-11

a. (1) Inventory Turnover = _____

_____

Current Year: _____

_____

Preceding Year: _____

_____

EXERCISE 17-11, Concluded

(2) Number of Days' Sales in Inventory = _____

_____

Current Year: _____

_____

Preceding Year: _____

_____

_____

_____

b. _____

_____

_____

_____

_____

_____

EXERCISE 17-12

a. (1) Inventory Turnover = _____

_____

Dell: _____

_____

HP: _____

_____

(2) Number of Days' Sales in Inventory = _____

_____

Dell: _____

_____

HP: _____

_____

_____

_____

EXERCISE 17-12, Concluded

b. _____

_____

_____

_____

_____

_____

_____

_____

_____

_____

_____

_____

_____

_____

_____

_____

_____

EXERCISE 17-13

a. Ratio of Liabilities to Stockholders' Equity = _____

_____

Dec. 31, 2012: _____

_____

Dec. 31, 2011: _____

_____

b. Number of Times Bond Interest Charges Are Earned = _____

_____

Dec. 31, 2012: _____

_____

Dec. 31, 2011: _____

_____

_____

_____

EXERCISE 17-13, Concluded

c. _____
_____
_____
_____
_____
_____

EXERCISE 17-14

a. Ratio of Liabilities to Stockholders' Equity = _____
_____

Hasbro: _____
_____

Mattel, Inc.: _____
_____

b. Number of Times Interest Charges Are Earned = _____
_____

Hasbro: _____
_____

Mattel, Inc.: _____
_____

c. _____
_____
_____
_____
_____
_____
_____
_____

EXERCISE 17-15

a. Ratio of Liabilities to Stockholders' Equity = _____

_____

H. J. Heinz: _____

_____

Hershey: _____

_____

b. Ratio of Fixed Assets to Long-Term Liabilities = _____

_____

H. J. Heinz: _____

_____

Hershey: _____

_____

c. _____

_____

_____

_____

_____

_____

_____

_____

_____

_____

_____

_____

_____

_____

_____

EXERCISE 17-16

a. Ratio of Net Sales to Total Assets = _____

_____

YRC Worldwide: _____

_____

Union Pacific: _____

_____

C. H. Robinson Worldwide Inc.: _____

_____

b. _____

_____

_____

_____

_____

_____

_____

_____

_____

_____

_____

_____

_____

_____

_____

_____

_____

_____

_____

_____

_____

_____

_____

_____

_____

_____

_____

_____

EXERCISE 17-17

a. Rate Earned on Total Assets = _____

_____

2012: _____

_____

_____

2011: _____

_____

_____

Rate Earned on Stockholders' Equity = _____

_____

2012: _____

_____

_____

2011: _____

_____

_____

Rate Earned on Common Stockholders' Equity = _____

_____

2012: _____

_____

_____

2011: _____

_____

_____

b. _____

_____

_____

_____

_____

_____

_____

_____

_____

EXERCISE 17-18

a. Rate Earned on Total Assets = _____

_____

Fiscal Year 2007: _____

_____

Fiscal Year 2006: _____

_____

b. Rate Earned on Stockholders' Equity = _____

_____

Fiscal Year 2007: _____

_____

Fiscal Year 2006: _____

_____

c. _____

_____

_____

_____

_____

_____

_____

d. _____

_____

_____

_____

_____

_____

_____

EXERCISE 17-19

a. Ratio of Fixed Assets to Long-Term Liabilities = _____

_____

_____

_____

_____

b. Ratio of Liabilities to Stockholders' Equity = _____

_____

_____

_____

_____

c. Ratio of Net Sales to Assets = _____

_____

_____

_____

_____

_____

_____

d. Rate Earned on Total Assets = _____

_____

_____

_____

_____

e. Rate Earned on Stockholders' Equity = _____

_____

_____

_____

_____

f. Rate Earned on Common Stockholders' Equity = _____

_____

_____

_____

_____

EXERCISE 17-20

a. Number of Times Bond Interest Charges Are Earned = _____

_____

_____

_____

_____

b. Number of Times Preferred Dividends Are Earned = _____

_____

_____

_____

_____

c. Earnings per Share on Common Stock = _____

_____

_____

_____

_____

d. Price-Earnings Ratio = _____

_____

_____

_____

_____

e. Dividends per Share of Common Stock = _____

_____

_____

_____

_____

f. Dividend Yield = _____

_____

_____

_____

_____

EXERCISE 17-21

a. Earnings per Share = _____

_____

_____

_____

_____

b. Price-Earnings Ratio = _____

_____

_____

_____

_____

c. Dividends per Share = _____

_____

_____

_____

_____

d. Dividend Yield = _____

_____

_____

_____

_____

EXERCISE 17-22

a. Price-Earnings Ratio = _____

_____

The Home Depot: _____

_____

Google: _____

_____

Coca-Cola: _____

_____

Dividend Yield = _____

_____

The Home Depot: _____

_____

Google: _____

_____

Coca-Cola: _____

_____

b. _____

_____

_____

_____

_____

_____

_____

_____

_____

_____

_____

_____

_____

_____

_____

_____

_____

_____

_____

_____

APPENDIX EXERCISE 17-23

a. Earnings per share on income before extraordinary items:

Earnings Before Extraordinary Items per Share on Common Stock = _____

_____

_____

_____

_____

_____

b. Earnings per Share on Common Stock = _____

_____

_____

_____

_____

APPENDIX EXERCISE 17-24

a. _____

b. _____

c. _____

d. _____

e. _____

f. _____

g. _____

APPENDIX EXERCISE 17-25

a.

Partial Income Statement		

b.

Partial Income Statement		

APPENDIX EXERCISE 17-26

a. _____
_____
_____
_____
_____
_____

b. _____
_____
_____
_____
_____
_____

PROBLEM 17-1 ___

1.

		2012	2011	INCREASE (DECREASE)	
				AMOUNT	PERCENT

Comparative Income Statement

2.

_____

_____

_____

_____

_____

_____

_____

_____

_____

_____

692

This Page Not Used.

PROBLEM 17-2 ___

1.

	Comparative Income Statement			
	2012		2011	
	AMOUNT	PERCENT	AMOUNT	PERCENT

2.

694

This Page Not Used.

PROBLEM 17-3 ___

1. a. Working Capital = _____

_____

_____

_____

_____

b. Current Ratio = _____

_____

_____

_____

_____

c. Quick Ratio = _____

_____

_____

_____

_____

PROBLEM 17-3 ___ , Concluded

2.

Transaction	Working Capital	Current Ratio	Quick Ratio
a.			
b.			
c.			
d.			
e.			
f.			
g.			
h.			
i.			
j.			

Supporting calculations:

Transaction	Current Assets	Quick Assets	Current Liabilities
a.			
b.			
c.			
d.			
e.			
f.			
g.			
h.			
i.			
j.			

PROBLEM 17-4 ___

1. through 19.

1. Working Capital: _____

Ratio	Numerator	Denominator	Calculated Value
2. Current ratio			
3. Quick ratio			
4. Accounts receivable turnover			
5. Number of days' sales in receivables			
6. Inventory turnover			
7. Number of days' sales in inventory			
8. Ratio of fixed assets to long-term liabilities			
9. Ratio of liabilities to stockholders' equity			
10. Number of times interest charges earned			
11. Number of times preferred dividends earned			
12. Ratio of net sales to assets			
13. Rate earned on total assets			
14. Rate earned on stockholders' equity			
15. Rate earned on common stockholders' equity			
16. Earnings per share on common stock			

PROBLEM 17-4 ___ , Concluded

Ratio	Numerator	Denominator	Calculated Value
17. Price-earnings ratio			
18. Dividends per share of common stock			
19. Dividend yield			

PROBLEM 17-5 ___

1. a.

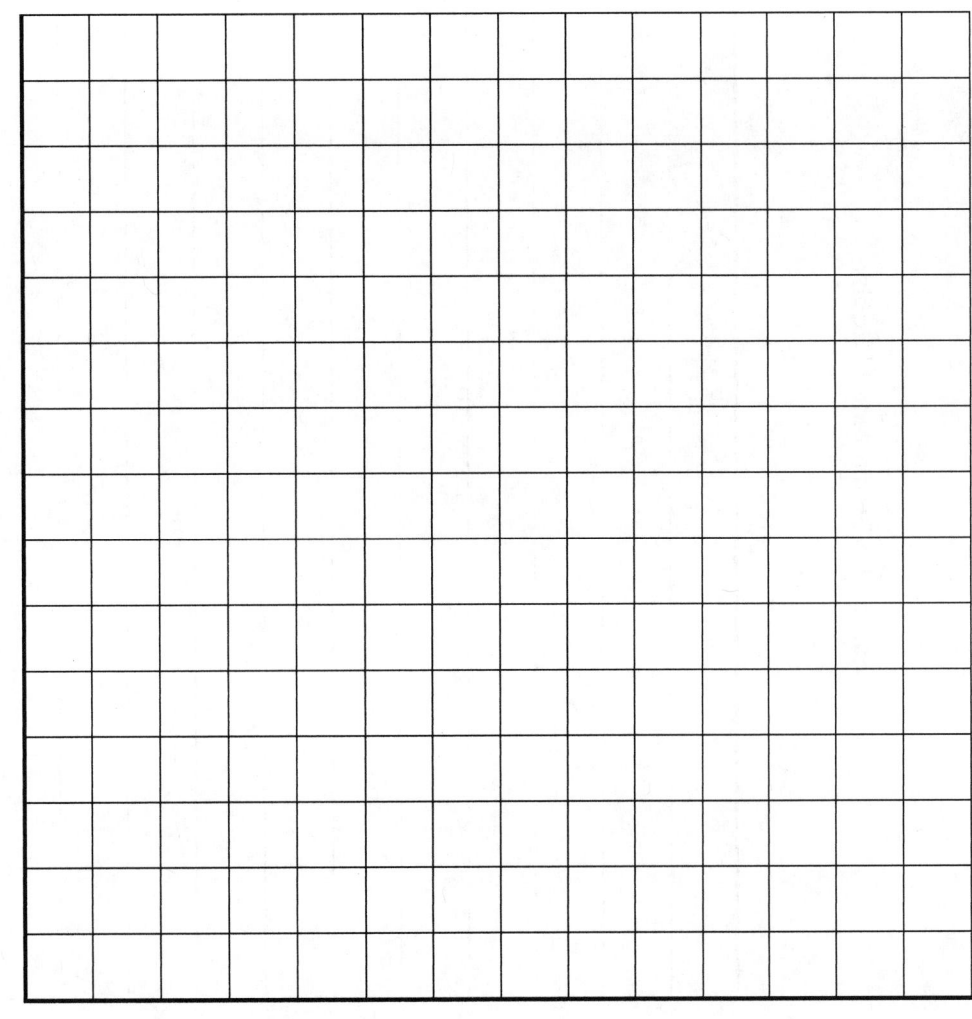

Year

Rate Earned on Total Assets = _____

_____

2012: _____   2009: _____

_____

2011: _____   2008: _____

_____

2010: _____

_____

PROBLEM 17-5 ___ , Continued

1. b.

Rate Earned on Stockholders' Equity

Year

Rate Earned on Stockholders' Equity = _____

_____

2012: _____   2009: _____

_____

2011: _____   2008: _____

_____

2010: _____

_____

PROBLEM 17-5 ___, Continued

1. c.

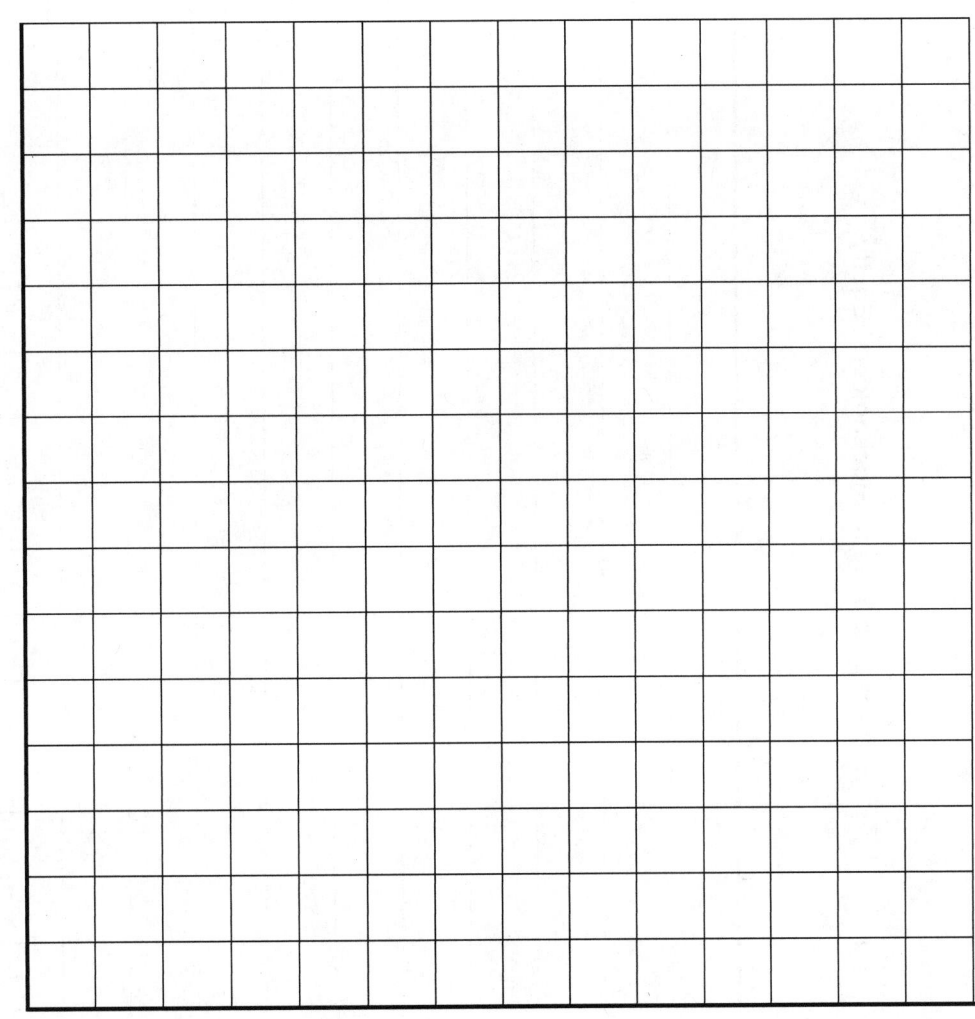

Number of Times Interest Charges Are Earned

Year

Number of Times Interest Charges Earned = _____

2012:		2009:
2011:		2008:
2010:		

PROBLEM 17-5 ___ , Continued

1. d.

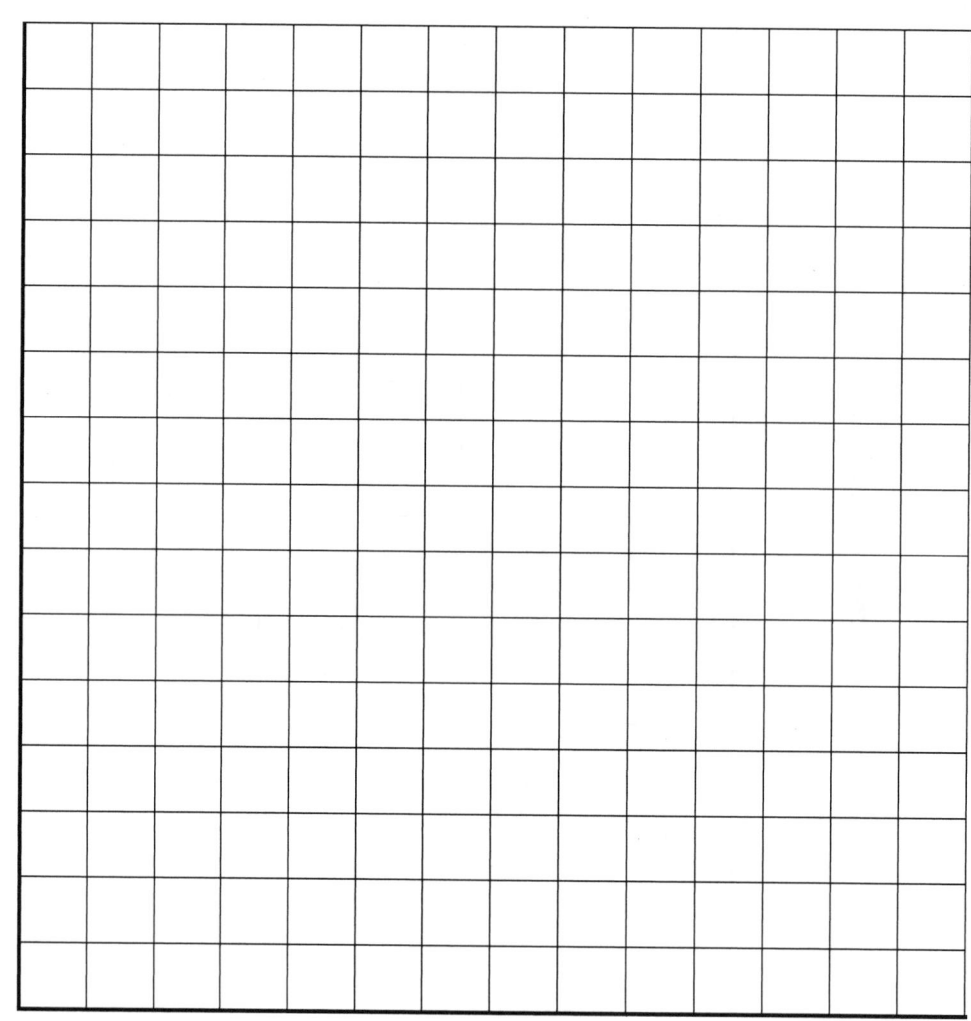

Ratio of Liabilities to Stockholders' Equity

Year

Ratio of Liabilities to Stockholders' Equity = _____

_____

2012: _____   2009: _____

_____

2011: _____   2008: _____

_____

2010: _____

_____

PROBLEM 17-5 ___, Concluded

2.

_____

_____

_____

_____

_____

_____

_____

_____

_____

_____

_____

_____

_____

_____

_____

_____

_____

_____

_____

_____

_____

_____

_____

_____

This Page Not Used.

NIKE, INC., PROBLEM

1. a. through m.

	2009	2008

NIKE, INC., PROBLEM, Continued

	2009	2008	

NIKE, INC., PROBLEM, Continued

2. a. through m.

_____

_____

_____

_____

_____

_____

_____

_____

_____

_____

_____

_____

_____

_____

_____

_____

_____

_____

_____

_____

_____

_____

_____

_____

_____

_____

_____

_____

_____

_____

_____

_____

_____

_____

_____

_____

_____

_____

NIKE, INC., PROBLEM, Concluded

EXERCISE B-1

a. and b.

JOURNAL

PAGE

	DATE		DESCRIPTION	POST. REF.	DEBIT	CREDIT	
1							1
2							2
3							3
4							4
5							5
6							6
7							7
8							8
9							9
10							10
11							11
12							12
13							13
14							14
15							15
16							16
17							17
18							18

EXERCISE B-2

a. and b.

JOURNAL

PAGE

	DATE		DESCRIPTION	POST. REF.	DEBIT	CREDIT	
1							1
2							2
3							3
4							4
5							5
6							6
7							7
8							8
9							9
10							10
11							11
12							12
13							13
14							14
15							15
16							16
17							17
18							18

EXERCISE B-3

a. (1) _____

   (2) _____

   (3) _____

   (4) _____

   (5) _____

b. (1) through (5)

JOURNAL   PAGE

	DATE		DESCRIPTION	POST. REF.	DEBIT	CREDIT	
1							1
2							2
3							3
4							4
5							5
6							6
7							7
8							8
9							9
10							10
11							11
12							12
13							13
14							14
15							15
16							16
17							17
18							18
19							19
20							20

EXERCISE B-4

a. (1) _____

   (2) _____

   (3) _____

   (4) _____

   (5) _____

b. (1) through (5)

JOURNAL

PAGE

	DATE	DESCRIPTION	POST. REF.	DEBIT	CREDIT	
1						1
2						2
3						3
4						4
5						5
6						6
7						7
8						8
9						9
10						10
11						11
12						12
13						13
14						14
15						15
16						16
17						17
18						18
19						19
20						20